Christopher Coker

Globalisation and Insecurity in the Twenty-first Century:

NATO and the Management of Risk

Adelphi Paper 345

Oxford University Press, Great Clarendon Street, Oxford OX2 6DP
Oxford   New York
Athens Auckland Bangkok Bombay Calcutta Cape Town
Dar es Salaam Delhi Florence Hong Kong Istanbul Karachi
Kuala Lumpur Madras Madrid Melbourne Mexico City
Nairobi Paris Singapore Taipei Tokyo Toronto
and associated companies in
Berlin Ibadan

Oxford is a trade mark of Oxford University Press

Published in the United States
by Oxford University Press Inc., New York

First published June 2002 by **Oxford University Press** for
The International Institute for Strategic Studies
Arundel House, 13–15 Arundel Street, Temple Place, London WC2R 3DX
www.iiss.org

Director John Chipman
Editor Mats R. Berdal
Assistant Editor John Wheelwright

British Library Cataloguing in Publication Data
Data available

Library of Congress Cataloguing in Publication Data

ISBN 0-19-851671-1
ISSN 0567-932x

Contents

Glossary

DIA	Defence Intelligence Agency
DoD	Department of Defence
EAPC	European Atlantic Partnership Council
ESDI	European Security and Defence Initiative
ICBLM	International Campaign to Ban Land Mines
IFOR	Implementation Force (Bosnia)
KLA	Kosovo Liberation Army
NATO	North Atlantic Treaty Organisation
NGO	Non-Government Organisation
NIC	National Intelligence Council
NSC	National Security Council
NWO	New World Order
OECD	Organisation of Economic Cooperation and Development
OSCE	Organisation for Security and Co-operation in Europe
PFP	Partnership for Peace
SECI	South-Eastern Europe Cooperation Initiative
UNDP	United Nations Development Program
UNHCR	United Nations High Commissioner for Refugees
UNICEF	United Nations Children's Fund
WHO	World Health Organisation
WTO	World Trade Organisation

Introduction

However much the term 'globalisation' has been criticized, no one has been able to dispense with it since it first gained general currency some twenty years ago.[1] It is now invoked as much by the policy community as by academics. It is not difficult to detect the Hegelian *Zeitgeist* hovering over this kind of thinking: the notion that there is a common spirit of the times discernible in all the activities of an age.

For a long time, however, globalisation was not discussed much, if at all, by the security community. Strategic concerns seemed remote from a world that had been conditioned to believe that the market was the source of contemporary history. The success with which the Western world achieved its material goals in the 1990s removed the impetus to enquire too deeply into the obverse side of globalisation: the discontents to which it gives rise and, even more, the strategies of the discontented. Just because war and its avoidance was the great topic of the twentieth century, many political economists argued, was no reason to expect that it would be of great interest in the twenty-first.

How quickly we forget the lessons of history, or the warnings it throws up. 'You may not be interested in war,' warned Leon Trotsky, 'but war is certainly interested in you'. This was as true for the victims of the 11 September World Trade Center attack as it was for the five million people who died in the many conflicts that raged across the world in the 1990s. In that sense, Trotsky may have been speaking for our age as well as his own – a sobering thought.

Taking this as its starting point, this Paper is divided into five chapters. In the first I attempt to define what globalisation is (no easy task, given the extensive literature and the extent of disagreement among scholars and policy-makers alike). Globalisation is important for its impact on a number of global systems, such as the global market, but the sum of these systems does not yet constitute a system itself. It also challenges institutions such as the state without threatening their continued existence. We still live in a system of nation states, even though they are being significantly transformed by transnational forces and challenges.

The second chapter looks at the debate on whether globalisation is transforming the nature of conflict itself. This is an argument that I find unconvincing. The causes of conflict are much the same as they were in the past and the world today is no more conflict-riven than it was before the Cold War came to an end. What is different, however, is that the world reacts to conflict very differently. What we are witnessing is the rise of a global civil society – a socially constructed and transnationally defined network of relationships between governments and non-government organisations (NGOs) that is giving the concerned citizen an opportunity for political involvement. For many citizens, especially in North America and Western Europe, the world is becoming the main frame of reference. Often public opinion demands that governments intervene with force in situations in which human rights are openly flouted. Sometimes, too, governments of their own volition seek to impose universal norms of civility.

In the third chapter I shall look at the new security agenda with which globalisation now confronts governments – especially those in Europe and North America, whose countries consider themselves members of a community called the West. Whether discussing the environment or nuclear proliferation, that community faces new challenges, or old challenges redefined by global events. 'Human security' is now of growing importance to the citizens of the Western world. So too is the need to manage risks that are potentially more catastrophic because they are global. Indeed, perhaps the most important feature of globalisation is the rise of risk communities, which now police risks and manage insecurity in their own distinctive fashion.

In the two concluding chapters I will try to place the Western world, and primarily NATO, in the context of globalisation. For new transnational factors are compelling it to work differently from the way it worked in the past, and new global sources of instability are compelling it to come to grips with such problems as terrorism as a transnational phenomenon. And, as a risk community (no longer the security community it was during the Cold War), the Alliance is confronted with the challenging problem of non-state actors and global networks, as opposed to the state-centric challenges of the past. NATO is only as strong as its member states, and they now find themselves increasingly sharing 'global governance' with non-state actors. An increasingly globalised world demands some form of global supervision. This is not the same as global government. It is in practical terms a case of governments recognizing that they share resources, structures and, above all, authority with non-state actors, especially NGOs.

Some of these challenges also have the potential to divide the Alliance, or to turn it into a 'virtual' community that is less than the sum of its parts. Although tensions between the United States and its European partners have been a characteristic of the Alliance for most of its history, past differences and divisions were always contained or managed – the discipline of the Cold War ensured this. In future, three dialectics of globalisation may make it increasingly difficult for the two sides to work together. The tensions between universal and local or regional forces, between transnational and national structures or states, and between pro-American and anti-American sentiments are all to be found within the Western world.

The conclusion of this Paper will set out some policy recommendations to help avoid that outcome. These will be focused on the central thesis of this Paper. Globalisation promises much, but it also makes people feel more insecure about the things they value most: their identity, their culture and the risks they are asked to face on a day-by-day basis. If globalisation is not to be found alienating, it requires a political response. NATO represents the most promising way of adapting security policy to the new global agenda. In every sphere, from terrorism to the defence of human rights, it can restore the primacy of politics over economics, the ultimate challenge that faces every political institution in the early twenty-first century.

Chapter 1

What is Globalisation?

As we have begun to use the term more frequently, the definition of globalisation has been increasingly contested. So too, according to one's perspective, its origins have been pushed back in time. The *cultural historian*, for example, who agrees with Geoffrey Barraclough that contemporary history begins when the problems that are actual in the world today first took visible shape, may want to trace the process back to the turn of the twentieth century. After all, the first book to talk of the 'Americanisation of the world' was published in 1902.

The *economist*, by comparison, may prefer to look back to the excess liquidity from consistent US balance-of-payments deficits in the 1960s and the subsequent collapse of the Bretton Woods fixed-rate regime, with its capital controls. Or he may choose to go back no further than the 1970s and the recycling of petrodollars, which resulted in an astonishingly high volume of foreign-exchange trading and speculative investment that dwarfed the currency reserves of governments and threatened to swamp the financial markets of individual nations. Today's annual foreign-exchange turnover is $300 trillion.[1]

As for the *political scientist*, he may detect real novelties in the increasing democratisation of the world. Since 1975, when Spain and Portugal rid themselves of their old dictatorships, the first ripple in a wave of democratisation has gathered momentum, spreading first to Latin America, then to Asia, and finally to Africa. Samuel Huntington has dubbed this 'the third wave' of global democratisation, comparing it with the first wave that swept Europe in the nineteenth century, and the second that appeared after the Second World War in much of the post-colonial world. The proportion of countries with some form of democratic government rose from 20% in 1974 to 61% in 1998.[2] And majority governments worldwide have now made legally binding commitments to respect the civil and political rights of their citizens. As people's participation in society has grown, so have the number of organisations that give it voice. And civic movements are forcing governments to engage and negotiate with society, field claims and pressures from diverse quarters and seek legitimacy by winning public approval for their performance.

The *security community* came to globalisation quite late in the day. In the 1990s it was confirmed in its belief that the world was getting safer for those who counted most: the countries that did well out of globalisation, largely because of the developments I have just sketched. The 'third wave of democratisation' comforted a community that believed that democracies do not go to war against each other. The increased complexity of financial transactions across the globe seemed to render war increasingly remote from power-policy concerns. 'Geo-economics' had allegedly displaced geopolitics, while economic wealth and 'soft' power were replacing violence and coercion as the ultimate currency of the 'global village'. And, culturally, the increased homogenisation of the world promised a future in which cultural identity (often the stimulus for conflict in the past) would matter less than before. Just because the world was riven by internecine conflicts in 'peripheral' areas, including the Balkans, seemed no reason to suspect that war, the predominant political theme of the twentieth century, would be even a major sub-theme of the twenty-first. Once the weapon of the strong, war now seemed to be the weapon of the weak.

It was not until twenty-two days into the Kosovo war that a major Western leader acknowledged that globalisation had a security dimension. Tony Blair's doctrine of 'international community', first adumbrated then in a speech in Chicago, acknowledged that all societies (whatever their different cultures) had to work together to sustain peace. 'We are all internationalists now,' he declared. It was a message that was given even greater urgency by the events of 11 September 2001. Both the Kosovo war and the attack on the World Trade Center appeared to reveal a unique dialectic at the heart of globalisation, between the global and the local. In many ways the dialectic is positive; it creates a synergistic tension between communities that brings them together, rather than forces them apart. It is also part of our post-modern discourse of 'difference'. 'Cultural borrowing', 'exchange', 'transfer', 'negotiation', 'acculturation', 'transculturation', 'hybridisation' – these are all part of the language of the hour, and they reveal the fragmentation of identity, especially national identity, under the impact of globalisation.

But in much of the world, claim some analysts, ethnic identities have given rise to ethnic wars, and the 'new' wars of the 1990s were different in character from the old. Our post-modern play with a variety of identities, writes Mary Kaldor, holds no sway over believers in a very narrowly prescriptive notion of group identity. Identity in many modern countries – and even more so in pre-modern countries – is still a matter of group identification. Many people around the world claim membership of a group or are claimed by a group, and often the encounter is a triumph of local particularism over the universalist message at the heart of the globalisation debate.

A second dialectic, which aroused even more interest and criticism, was Samuel Huntington's claim that identities based on different values and norms were likely to be the chief characteristic of our globalised age. Globalisation exacerbates societal and ethnic consciousness. The global religious revival, 'the return of the sacred', is a response to peoples' perceptions of the world as 'a single space'. In such a world, writes Huntington, the most urgent task is 'to prevent the escalation of major inter-civilisational conflicts into major inter-civilisational wars'. Though largely discredited when it was first advanced, Huntington's thesis has come back into play with Al-Qaeda's attack on the United States.

For Pierre Hassner, a third dialectic is that between the 'bourgeois' and the 'barbarian', the latter being defined as movements or groups that, far from sparing civilians, now target them directly through genocide (Rwanda), ethnic cleansing (Kosovo) or terrorism (World Trade Center). War no longer revolves primarily around the rivalry between states; it revolves around conflicts between societies that globalisation brings into closer contact than ever before. The old idea of war – of soldier fighting soldier and state competing with state – has largely been discredited; in its place the state finds itself fighting barbarians in many shapes: bandits, militiamen, *mafiosi*, mercenaries, and warlords.[3] And crime and terrorism are fuelled by other global challenges that are shaping the Western security agenda, such as inequalities of wealth and the proliferation of weapons of mass destruction.

What all three dialectics appear to suggest is that the 'local' is the main source of conflict in a globalised era. Although distant geographically, the local and global – the two worlds of 'peace' and 'war' – are in constant interaction through organised crime and global terrorist networks, and through patterns of migration, as millions of people are forced to leave their countries of origin to escape failing states, and even failing regions of the globe. From the purely technical point of view, the worlds of the *Tomahawk* cruise missile and the AK-47 (the non-state actor's weapon of choice) are increasingly converging. In our global age cultures encounter each other and interpenetrate more than ever before.

But, while it is plausible to argue that all three dialectics produce conflict, this is not necessarily so. The debate is not helped by the fact that many of the leading analysts of conflict have an imperfect understanding of globalisation itself. We need a more complex understanding of its main features if we are to understand the nature of contemporary conflict, as well as the security challenges to which it gives rise. The dialectic between the global and local is merely one dialectic among many – globalisation itself is a dialectical process. Ethnicity does not always define nationality, any more than race or class. Ethnicity may fuel conflicts, but rarely does it cause them to break out. Cultural differences, though important, are more fluid than ever before as cultures are more interpenetrated. And the barbarians are often *within* the gates, waiting to break out rather than to break in.

Global, Globalism, Globalisation

Sociologists have used different criteria to describe globalisation, and it is they who have tended to determine the terms of the debate, because they have written at length about our own times: the way we ourselves think about the events and processes which are shaping and reshaping our lives. Yet even among sociologists, who have invoked the term globalisation the most, 'global' was still being used primarily in the sense of 'total' as recently as the late 1970s. Indeed, as an accepted term it only entered their vocabulary in the early 1990s. By then it had come to convey a widespread sense of the transformation of the world.

And yet, even between sociologists, there is still no general agreement on what is being transformed. We need, therefore, to distinguish globalisation from globalism, and both from the global world in which we have lived for so long.

The *global* contrasts with the national. It evokes the global environment or habitat in which humanity lives. It involves the idea of holism: namely that the habitat, social or environmental, constitutes a unity. In the nineteenth century the world went global for the first time. Compound nouns with 'world' first began to appear in the lexicons of the time: 'world politics', 'world economy', 'world trade', 'world power', 'world empire', 'world protection', 'world order' and most ambitious of all, 'world history'.

As Marx tells us in *Introduction to a Critique of Political Economy* (1857) 'world history did not always exist; history as world history [wa]s a result' of the international division of labour which the industrial revolution introduced.[4] Business activity, in particular, broadened individual activity into 'world-historical activity'. And the 'global', of course, involved more than economics. The 'Contemporary Politics' course offered at the University of Wisconsin by Paul Reinsch in the academic year 1899–1900 was the first course of its kind anywhere in the United States to deal specifically with the subject matter of world politics.[5] The subject matter expanded in the period 1870–1920 as a result of the inclusion of some non-European societies (Japan) in the international system; a sharp increase in the number and forms of global communication; the rise of ecumenical movements; the development of global competitions (the Olympics); and the League of Nations. But it was the world wars, of course, and the Cold War that followed, that established in the minds of many strategists the fact that they lived in a global age.

The 'global', therefore, is not a project but a process. If it is always threatening to transcend the nation state as a focus of analysis, the nation state still remains one of the principal units of account. No single global system has emerged. We are likely to witness many global experiences or encounters. There are likely to be many local situations responsive to global pressures or conflicts, and many encounters between particular peoples prompted by global events.

This was another of Marx's insights, for he was the first writer to note how a new technological development in Britain could destroy entire livelihoods in China or India in a single year. These actions were not intended, and his insight was that the growth of the world market exposed an increasing percentage of the world population to unintended, long-distance harm. A double revolution was taking place. Old types of deliberate harm, caused by warring states and expanding empires, were gradually being replaced by diffuse forms of harm transmitted across frontiers by the forces of global capitalism. The market, and not only war or politics, was reshaping the world. The market differed from the imperial orders of the past; and the market mechanism differed from war. As a result, an extended sense of moral responsibility to the human race (or globalism) began to emerge.[6]

Globalism contrasts with nationalism, just as the global contrasts with the national. Just as nationalism preached the virtues of the nation state, so globalism preaches the virtues of the global. The twentieth century saw the rise of three globalist philosophies: Marxism, liberalism and radical (or political) Islam (or Islamicism). All three promised to liberate humanity (or their own followers) from oppression or social alienation. All three tried to engage in what Zygmunt Bauman calls 'history by design'.[7] Globalism will continue as a force despite the collapse of Marxism – which, in retrospect, can be seen as merely a failed form of it. With its demise, of course, only two movements are now left.

Islamicist movements were active in the Middle East as early as the 1930s and 1940s, even if they spread a little more slowly than is the case today. Their members were as consciously global then as they are now, fixing on the West as their main target and attempting to promote a universal message against Western dominance.[8] Yet many of these movements divided the Islamic community as well. For the encounter between Islam and modernity pitted those who saw democracy as a universal ideal – to be achieved through the Muslim idea of *shura* (consultation) and *ijma* (consensus) – against those who saw democracy and the faith as incompatible – because in a democracy sovereignty lies with the people, whereas in Islam it lies with God.

This tension increased as the twentieth century unfolded. Indeed, back in 1991 some writers predicted that the North–South struggle would displace the old conflict between East and West. Ali Mazrui argued that Islam had potent weapons in that conflict: the petrodollar against the West; demographic growth against Russia; and today perhaps a third factor can be added, terrorism.[9] Only fifteen years later this crude analysis looks rather unconvincing. Mazrui's mistake was to see conflict in inter-state terms. For non-state actors are in the van of radical Islam.

The majority, of course, are not transnational, despite links with similar movements in neighbouring countries. But some, like Al-Qaeda, are truly global in their reach. The movement's cells were to be found at one time in 60 countries, part of a complex of connections embedded in countries but linked between and across societies. The assassins responsible for the death of the Afghan warlord Ahmed Shah Masood before the 11 September attack on the United States were Algerians with Belgian passports, whose visas to enter Pakistan had been issued in London. Masood's death shows how radical Islam does not reject the means of globalisation, only its message. Islamism indeed thrives on globalisation: on Saudi and Gulf-state funding for mosque-building programmes and the rapid spread of information and communications technology. Both empower the *ummah* (the world-wide Muslim community). But, for radical Islam (as opposed to the mainstream Muslim world), the message is different; its followers wish to construct, not a Kantian cosmopolitan order, but a world order (*al nizam al-islami*) based on fundamentalist values and the duty of *jihad* (religious war).

The spectacle of Islamic radicals wrestling with the past may be more arresting than that of humanitarians engaging with the future, but for the moment humanitarianism is the stronger of the two globalist forces. The nineteenth century was the first to invent the concept of human rights, and with these came the concept of a collective crime: a crime against humanity. The Enlightenment taught that all men were equal, so to avoid the charge of criminality states had to dehumanise their enemies, to exclude them from the human race (Jews, class enemies). In 1945 that strategy was made illegitimate by the Allied powers at Nuremberg and by the Universal Declaration of Human Rights (1948), which was signed by all the victors including the Soviet Union. As Michael Ignatieff contends, writing of the famine in Ethiopia in the 1980s:

> *If we take it for granted now that the Ethiopians are our responsibility it is because a century of total destruction has made us ashamed of that cantonment of moral responsibilities by nation, religion or region, which resulted in the abandonment of the Jews. Modern universalism is built upon the emergence of a new kind of crime: the crime against humanity.*[10]

Humanitarianism is the most appealing globalist force today. Yet its belief in universal values and norms sits uneasily with radical Islam's particularist message, which insists on the norms and values of the *ulaama* or Muslim brotherhood. As Ignatieff concludes, 'We in the West start from a universalist ethics based on ideas of human rights; they start from particularist ethics that define the tribe, the nation or ethnicity as the limit of legitimate concern'. It was that Western belief that spurred global civil society to demand intervention from the international community in Somalia and Bosnia in the 1990s: the great era of peacekeeping operations. A collective crime is now deemed to demand a collective response.

Globalisation binds the syntax of the global and its derivation 'globalism' into a process which involves nothing less than the transformation of the world. If the global is the sum of multiple local activities with worldwide range, consequences and significance, then globalisation involves the interpenetration of local activities with world-wide range, consequence and significance.

Unlike globalism, however, globalisation is not a project. It has no programme. It refers in the first place to the many different complex patterns of interconnectiveness and interdependence that have arisen in the late twentieth century. It has implications for all spheres of social existence: the economic, the political, and even the military. In all three it ties local life to global structures, processes and events.

Looking first at the economic implications of these enmeshing links, we may not yet live in a single world society, but every aspect of social reality is simultaneously undergoing globalisation. Witness the emergence of a world economy, a cosmopolitan culture, and the rise of international social movements. And this global interconnectedness runs much deeper than the interdependence of states discussed in the 1950s, when academics identified for the first time the rise of transnational organisations such as multinational corporations.

One the most striking examples is international crime. The money-laundering operations conducted through the infamous Bank of Credit and Commerce International linked 32 separate national financial systems and contributed significantly to the globalisation of crime. Today organised crime is now transnational: all the main syndicates or cartels operate and are structured internationally. And their other activities exacerbate other global problems. They sustain international terrorist movements; they are involved in the smuggling of uranium, which facilitates the dissemination of weapons of mass destruction; and they are deeply involved in the illegal trafficking of people, which adds another dimension to the challenge of migration.

Then there is the legitimate economy. In 2000 more money was traded on the world money markets than the World Bank has lent in its entire history.[11] Today's financial markets have broken out of their geographical constraints; they have escaped the territorial framework that defined most banking, securities, derivatives and insurance markets before 1960. In addition, the integration of capital and commodity markets since the 1970s has surpassed all previous levels and is still spreading.

In the security field globalisation has also restructured international society as well as the way we think about security itself.

For the main challenge to states comes not from other states seeking to improve their geostrategic position but from non-state actors with whom global governance is increasingly shared, or with whom states now often find themselves in conflict.

Turning to the political implications of this trend, globalisation also involves an increasing awareness of global interconnectedness. It fosters the consciousness of the world as a single frame of reference. Global theorists like Roland Robertson have emphasized the ways in which the language of globalisation captures the increasingly widespread conscious awareness of the interdependence of local ecologies, economies and societies.[12] An embryonic global civil society is beginning to emerge which wishes to police international norms or values, and to intervene to alleviate human suffering. Whether we consider ourselves members of that society or not, we have to have a view of it, and that view (depending on how globalised our society is) will be determined by the very process we are analysing.

Any definition of globalisation, however, presents us with a dilemma. Indeed, the word itself presents us with two problems: the first is the 'global'; the second is the '-isation'. The implication of the first is that a single system of connection, notably through capital and commodity markets and information flows and imagined landscapes (global civil society), has penetrated the entire globe; the implication of the second is that it is doing so now; that we have already entered a 'global age'. Neither proposition is true.

Instead, what we are witnessing is the impact of globalisation on a series of existing global systems, such as the global market and global politics. The sum of these systems does not yet constitute a system itself.[13] Instead, we should see globalisation as a process that transforms without eradicating the institutions and features of the political landscape in which it is at work. It does not entail the end of territorial geography or territoriality or supra-territoriality: these still co-exist in complex inter-relationships. It may be changing the nature of social structures, such as the state and the nation, but neither the state nor the nation have been replaced.

Secondly, not everyone is living through the global age. If Renato Ruggiero, the first Director General of the World Trade Organization (WTO), was right to describe globalisation as a reality which 'overwhelms all others' we must still ask how 'real' it is for many people.[14] For the impact of globalisation has been unequal: greater in the North than the South; in the younger generation than the older; in the professional class than manual workers. It is expected that Internet access through computers and cellular phones will increase from 2.5% of the world's population today to 30% by 2010; but, of the 70% of the world not connected by that date, about half will never have made a phone call.[15]

At present the gap between the globalised and the un-globalised is the greatest of all cultural divisions. It is much more profound than any 'fault lines' between civilisations, for it cuts across age, class and gender. Neither side understands the other. To the globalised the other seems marginal; to the marginal, the globalised appear uncaring and exploitative. This difference is likely to be a growing source of conflict in the near future.

Even the intellectual community often fails to bridge the gap, despite the power of the imagination. The publication of Salman Rushdie's novel *The Satanic Verses* involved the EU in a confrontation with Iran. It is an excellent example of an issue that was caused by globalisation, but one that also reveals the extent to which the world is still unglobalised. Rushdie's novel was an example of a post-modern Western cultural genre (satire, which looks back to Swift and even earlier). Western intellectuals recognised the genre but not the culture (the Koran). Islamic intellectuals recognised the culture but not the genre.

In the end, globalisation is ambiguous, which is why it promotes insecurity. It creates wealth, but it also creates inequalities. It maximises opportunities, but it also maximises risks. We are not sure whether globalisation is 'enabling' or 'disempowering'. It is a *dialectical* process that is necessarily ambiguous, because we stand not at its end but at its beginning.

Hence, anything we conclude about the process of globalisation must in the nature of things be provisional. All we know is that, while it offers the globalised hope of a more secure future or a world increasingly in tune with itself, it also makes many peoples, nations and societies who feel marginalised increasingly insecure, and in some cases predisposed to violence.

Chapter 2

War, Globalisation and Global Civil Society

There is a tendency to divide the world into those who have 'made it' (the globalised), and those who have not (the local), which is merely another way of distinguishing the 'haves' from the 'have-nots'. It is also argued by some that the ethnic and other conflicts that have proliferated since the end of the Cold War should be seen as the product of 'alienation' from globalisation, just as creeds such as fascism can be seen as consolation for those who in the twentieth century found themselves alienated from modernity. Finally, it is claimed that even the form that many wars now take, particularly the propensity to target civilians, has transformed war into 'atrocity management' or 'conspicuous destruction'. In a word, under the impact of globalisation, wars are now 'new'.

None of these arguments is necessarily true, and some are distinctly unconvincing. We must go back to my definition of globalisation: the extent to which it promotes global interconnectedness, and the extent to which it promotes global consciousness: the belief that what happens in one part of the world should be of interest to the rest of it.

To take the first argument, in their book *The Real World Order* (1991) Max Singer and Aaron Wildawsky write:

> *The key to understanding the real world order is to separate the two into two parts. One part is zones of peace, wealth and democracy. The other is zones of turmoil, war and development.*

On the whole they are optimistic. Appropriately, their book is dedicated to the memory of Herman Kahn, the futurist of the 1960s and 1970s, well-known for his bold, often unorthodox and largely positive views on coming events. Saluting their mentor, they claim that 'he would have gloried in the world's brilliant prospects'. The thrust of their own view is clearly set forth in the opening paragraph of their introduction: 'whether this book is optimistic or pessimistic depends on whether a century is a short time or a long time'.[1]

In brief, they believe that the violence and disorder that characterises much of the world today may be transitional. Like many political economists, they find the zone of peace of much greater historical significance than the zone of war. The world may be violent, but it is less dangerous to those that matter most: the countries of the post-industrial world.

Ironically, this global framework rests on the premise that there has been a 'military *deglobalisation*' of the globe: a process that contrasts markedly with the period between 1914 and 1991, which saw two world wars and the arms build-up of the cold-war era. The Cold War militarised the planet as no other conflict had. Not only did it establish a nuclear regime that could have enabled the superpowers to destroy each other (and much of the world) in 30 minutes; it also saw an immense increase in the trading of arms and the spread of proxy wars. By the end of the conflict, Europe was the most heavily armed part of the planet, just as it had been in 1914.[2]

Military deglobalisation, by contrast, can be said to have been a feature of the post-1991 world. Annual military expenditures are down from their peak (1987), and military manpower levels for the industrial world are now the lowest in a century. And something more marks the zone of peace: the rise of supra-territoriality. This, argues Jan Scholte, has generally reduced incentives for war, particularly in the democracies, where globalisation has had its deepest impact.[3] War threatens the global circulation of capital and complicates global management of the biosphere and the environment. Violence can no longer be used effectively as an instrument of policy between post-industrial states or post-modern countries. It is the poor who resort to war; by one calculation a poor country is 85 times more likely to experience violent conflict than a rich one.[4]

Accelerated military deglobalisation, however, has not created post-military states in much of the world; on the contrary it has encouraged the inward application of force by the state. According to the UN Development Programme (UNDP), 61 civil conflicts disfigured the face of global politics between 1989 and 1999. Armed forces across the world have repressed ethnic minorities and created a new market for the out-sourcing of war. And the zone of peace is not disengaged from the zone of war. Far from it; the two zones' interaction has produced a new climate of insecurity in the form of 'leaking misery' (refugees); 'entrepreneurial misery' (crime) and political discontent (terrorism).

And what is happening in the zone of disorder? Drawing on her own experience travelling through war-ridden Bosnia, Mary Kaldor paints the picture of 'new wars' that differ from the old not only in their goals and methods of financing, but also in their ultimate cause: state failure. Globalisation has shattered state structures, divided societies along cultural fault lines and pitted citizen against citizen in a battle between tolerance and extremism – between those who hold on to the belief in multicultural societies and those who believe in the politics of fragmentation. In the response to globalisation and its effects, identity politics has replaced the ideological politics of the past.

> *The upsurge in the politics of particularist identities has to be explained in the context of a growing dissonance between those who participate in globalisation and those who are excluded.*[5]

In short, she claims, globalisation stimulates war among those who are alienated from it.

But does it do more? Has it changed the traditional character of war? Kaldor thinks so, and argues that the 'new wars' are distinct from the old, the 'Clausewitzian wars' or 'wars of classical modernity'. William Zartman writes that state failure is a process, not an event: a process akin 'to a long term degenerative disease'.[6] And globalisation, contends Martin Shaw, makes for 'degenerate war', waged by groups with no clear objectives or political ideology.[7] Thus, in Bosnia all sides relied on irregulars and special units, whose ill-discipline was legendary and whose motivation was greed, profit, and not ethnic consciousness. Eighty-three such groups were identified in Croatia and Bosnia in the early 1990s. These irregulars were later co-opted into armies and militias, and violence was brought under state control. In the Balkans they were used quite deliberately by political leaders to spread terror and disorder.

The problem, writes Mats Berdal, is that the 'distinctive characteristics' of new wars turns out on closer inspection to be neither distinctive nor very new. Moreover, in essence, the claim is another articulation of a theme popular among anti-globalisation protesters – the death of *the political*. Globalisation, writes one French writer, has led 'to a violence whose expressions are numerous but dispersed, disarticulated and without political expression'.[8] Of Colombia another analyst writes that violence has led to the erosion of the political dimension as crime cartels have taken over.[9] Another claims that the *Aum Shinrikyo* sect in Japan, which launched a chemical attack on the Tokyo subway in 1995, was engaged in a violence that is 'metapolitical'.[10] Wars, it is claimed, are now directed primarily against civilians, waged by parties and elements of decomposing state systems, often in the name of ethnic or tribal politics. Globalisation, add others, is leading to the 'rebarbarisation' of large parts of the world; it threatens 'the Lebanisation of national states, in which culture is pitted against culture, people against people and tribe against tribe'.[11]

John Keegan has given the argument a historical spin by comparing our modern times with the past. The sixteenth and seventeenth centuries saw the state assert its monopoly of force by disarming local warlords and feudal retainers, the hired hands and mercenaries and private armies that had been such a feature of the medieval world. In the nineteenth century Western imperialism required the disarming of the tribes, clans and martial races of the world. Today, Keegan argues, the tribes are reappearing and reasserting their right to arms. Clans and militias have returned, and warlords have emerged from the wings. And the West? It has neither the will, nor the resources, nor, above all, the 'cultural ruthlessness' to disarm them.[12]

The problem is that the idea of a 'world disorder' in which a zone of permanent instability is juxtaposed to a zone of peace is largely a myth, at least as regards the first. To begin with, it is not true that there are more local wars than in the past. SIPRI estimates that, on the global scale, the number of full-scale wars both within and between countries has actually decreased in recent years. In only two regions, Europe and the Middle East, has the number risen; in Asia, Africa and the Americas, meanwhile, it has remained constant or fallen quite significantly. If we take a long historical perspective, the high point of civil wars in the twentieth century was the age of national liberation in the 1960s and early 1970s.

And even if we apply a different measurement, not the number of wars but the number of those killed in them, the casualty list (at least in terms of fatalities) in wars in Croatia, Bosnia, Kosovo, Chechnya, Nagorno Karabakh, Tajikistan, Moldova and Georgia is half a million – less than the number killed in several individual conflicts during the Cold War. And many of the conflicts that are now raging can be traced back to that conflict, such as the wars in Angola, Cambodia, Sudan and Afghanistan, which between them have notched up over 3.5 million casualties. As Charles King writes, even if we add Rwanda (800,000) or the million lost in the Congo since 1996, the numbers are modest by comparison with the tally of those who lost their lives in every decade of the Cold War.[13]

So, if the situation is not quite as bleak as many people imagine, why do we think it is? Why are we more sensitive to global violence than we were in the past? Why do governments sometimes feel compelled to intervene in distant conflicts? The main explanation is to be found in the rise of global consciousness – and in this case that of a global civil society whose origins predate the end of the Cold War. Globalisation has not engendered greater violence, but it has promoted greater interest and moral engagement on the part of a global citizenry which is more aware of the wars that are being fought and which insists on the articulation of global norms. And, where those norms are in danger or challenged, it demands intervention.

Global Civil Society

When did the idea, rather than reality, of global civil society arise? It arose first in the early nineteenth century in the British Empire, an institution which was not only driven by state interests but also by those of trading companies, as well as extensive missionary activity and good works. And no issue taxed the British conscience more than the slave trade.

The anti-slavery movement was the first global protest movement in history. And it is interesting that *The Economist* came out against attempts to suppress the trade for a host of reasons, many of which it used more recently in its argument for decriminalising drugs. In the case of the slave trade, the journal contended, suppression was futile (efforts stopped at most 10 per cent of the commerce). It was also costly (many sailors' lives were lost needlessly); the effort to make the trade illegal led to corruption at the point of origination and destination of the cargo; and attempts to stop the trade had led to political destabilisation in the originating countries. Finally, attempts to stop the traffic had greatly increased the suffering of the very people those efforts were meant to help. The solution was to decriminalise the trade and regulate it more strictly.[14]

The Economist presented a powerful case on behalf of a powerful lobby for the re-legalisation of slavery. The problem with its argument was that most of what it said was true and universally recognised at the time. Even the abolitionists admitted that Africans in illegal slave ships were treated worse than if they had been shipped under a legal trade. As for the longevity of slavery it is still with us; it only became universally illegal in 1982, when it was banned by Mali, and it is still widespread enough in practice in both traditional and new forms to keep the NGO Anti-slavery International very busy indeed. In the end, the answer of the abolitionists who were too stubborn to be won over by rational argument was that the slave trade and slavery were evils.

In other words, the first global protest movements were sustained by moral fervour, as many are today, but they were also sustained by missionary zeal within the reach of British power, the *Pax Britannica*. Indeed, by the end of the nineteenth century the humanitarian impulse extended to the idea of trusteeship and humanitarian imperialism. What is different today is that the humanitarian impulse is almost entirely secular, and global civil society is no longer conceived within empires; nor is it directed by a powerful state. It flourishes in the absence of a global state or world empire.

Governments are still important for that reason, as regulators and members of international regulative authorities such as the IMF and the WTO: the very institutions that their own citizens now protest against. But governments now share *governance*. Indeed, the emergence of 'global governance' has made the international system less government-centred. International organisations have developed into 'global governance agencies' with a certain independence from states. Global corporations and civil-society actors have also become instrumental in the regulation of the international intergovernment order (witness the German government's cooperation with Greenpeace in its attempt to prosecute Brent Spar for dumping oil in the North Sea).

Commentators have begun to speak of 'international non-government organisations', 'trans-national advocacy networks', and 'global social movements'. Global civil society feeds on the work of charities and citizen protest groups, as well as that of small and large corporations. Over the past three decades there has been an explosion in the number of NGOs, while the deregulation of domestic economies and the strengthening of international economic regimes has allowed for a parallel explosion of multinational companies, banks, service networks and economic associations. There are now some 40,000 non-profit international, non-governmental organisations. They disburse more money than the United Nations (excluding the World Bank and the IMF) and are responsible for disbursing two-thirds of the European Union's relief aid. In recent years we have also seen the participation of NGOs in election-monitoring, and in Kosovo the involvement of 100 or more in the government of the country.

Yet the fact that this society has emerged in the absence of a global government, or of global empires like the British – the fact that it has arisen instead under 'lawless' conditions – contains within it a pressing constitutional agenda: the urgent need to develop a rule of law on a global scale.[15] For there is no central global government and not even a central international system, only a Holy Roman Empire hotchpotch of different jurisdictions – a cluster of nation states and regional governments; intergovernment institutions, some with responsibility over sectors (WTO and trade); international organisations seeking to enforce the rule of law globally (International Court of Justice); and a series of global accords and treaties. As John Keane argues, this is a structure, not a system, yet it is slowly eroding the immunity of sovereign states from legal prosecution and the presumption that statutes do not extend to the territory of other states.

And the informed citizen is much better informed than his nineteenth-century counterpart, thanks to technologies that allow him to monitor different-sized public spheres, some of them global, in which millions of people witness globalised debates on inequality and human rights. Thanks to that technology the public practice of non-violently monitoring the exercise of power across borders has begun to take root.[16] Geostationary satellites, digital media, the growth of giant information firms like CNN and News Corp., and the development of new technologies such as the Internet are all making it impossible to remain cultural relativists – to say with Pascal that essentially good and evil are a question of latitude.[17]

Take just one of those technologies: the Internet. Manuel Castells uses a historical analogy to explain its growing significance. The growth of labour movements in the industrial era cannot be divorced from the industrial factory as its organisational setting. So, too, the Internet is not simply a technology; it is the material infrastructure of a given organisational form: the network. The anti-globalisation movement is an electronic network, an Internet-based movement. The Internet has become the indispensable medium of the new social networks that have emerged in the network communities that are at the heart of global civil society.[18]

And global civil society is also beginning to determine the terms of the debate about war as well – thanks to technology, the public practise of monitoring the exercise of power across borders has begun to take root. The informed citizen is debating how, when and where to use force, and he is doing so in the context not so much of war as of global policing.

No wonder that many governments too have begun to see war in much the same terms as global civil society. War is no longer an 'act of will' (in the Clausewitzian sense of the term) so much as an activity directed against those who have turned war into crime. This was seen first in the attempt in 1989 to arrest General Manuel Noriega and forcibly extradite him from Panama for trial in the United States. The next example was America's attempt to arrest the Somali warlord Mohammed Farah Aideed under a warrant issued by the Security Council. In Haiti, the United States was sent in to exercise police powers. In Kosovo the action was directed against a 'criminal regime'. The most recent action is the war against terror, which, in the case of Al-Qaeda, took the form of an international manhunt for the world's Public Enemy No. 1.

Sometimes the contemplated action is quite literally police work (arresting suspects and targeting others). Sometimes the rhetoric of policing is intended to reassure public opinion that the forces are only engaged in policing – as though, writes Kenneth Anderson, this was somewhat less dangerous than war. The trouble is that this threatens to *de-politicise* the use of military force. In dismissing the Serb army in Kosovo as thugs, criminals or gangs like the Cripps or Bloods in East LA, it devalues politics, for the great majority of today's soldiers are still motivated by political interests and agendas. The other problem is that it tries to revalue war by turning it into policing, which is also dangerous. For there is an enormous difference between a police force and an army. First, in terms of firepower, police are armed with light weapons, because public order can only be policed that way. Military power exists to destroy military forces, and, although more precise and more lethal than in the past, weapons of war will always involve collateral damage.[19] Secondly, adds Anderson, while the fundamental task of the military is to destroy forces in the field, the fundamental task of the police is to stop criminal behaviour and bring the guilty to justice; their primary responsibility is to apprehend and arrest criminals, not to take them out. This distinction is likely to prove a constant source of misunderstanding and tension between Western governments and global civil society in future.

For the moment, however, the importance of global civil society and its conventions and regimes is that questions such as human rights are no longer subsumed into questions of power but into questions of international conscience. By its very nature, the human-rights agenda of the United States in the Cold War years was really an attempt to translate the rules of power into a form of procedure for the adoption of human rights themselves (that, after all, was the role of war: to make the world 'safe for democracy'). Human rights, however, cannot be imposed, nor can they be tools of government for managing society. They must emerge from a dialogue between governments and (increasingly) between governments and non-state actors. The success of Charter 77, and the increasing pressure that the Soviet Union faced because of its human-rights record in the closing years of the Cold War, show how governments can fall victim to the dialogue between cultures that global civil society makes possible.

Even the West has changed. It has been forced to recognise the struggle for equal sovereignty, the anti-colonial revolution, the principle of racial equality, the drive for economic justice and cultural liberation. There have been vast changes in Western attitudes since the 1950s, which include public attitudes towards the equal rights of non-Western states, national liberation from colonial rule, equal rights of non-white races, the rights of poor people to economic justice and cultural autonomy. Dialectically, the West has been forced – in Hedley Bull's phrase – to 'become free', both internally and in its relations with others

Of course, we can still only glimpse the character of a true 'global civil society', one centred less on the nation state and more on the concept of world citizenship. It would be a society distinguished not by its 'time zones' or levels of development, but by a truer sense of belonging to a common whole. And when (and if) it is realised, it will be more feasible to build new coalitions of interest or conscience around issues of justice which transcend the nation state and race, just as the nation state and race once transcended these issues. It is just about possible to imagine a world order in which there will be one global conversation, with limited participation open to all, but probably full participation open to none. The larger NGOs have more than anyone else articulated a yearning for such an order. The future may not be theirs, but they have set its agenda.

Chapter 3

Globalisation and the New Security Agenda

In March 1933 a new patient came to Freud. She was an American poet, Hilda Doolittle, better known to us by her pen-name HD. The clouds of Nazism hung heavy over Europe that spring. Severely traumatised by the First World War, HD was frightened. She came to Freud, 'in order to fortify and equip myself to face war when it came'; she came to calm, as she wrote in her book, *Tribute to Freud*, '[her] own personal little dragon of war terror'.[1]

Today most of us are no longer haunted by the fear of war in what Carl Sagan called our 'demon-haunted world': the fear that drove Doolittle to Freud, the fear that led WH Auden to describe the twentieth century as 'an age of anxiety'. None of us seem to fear war between the major powers. Instead our anxieties lead us to fight other wars: the 'war against crime', the 'war against poverty', the 'war against terrorism', the 'war on drugs'. It is significant that we prefer to use the word 'war', if at all, to describe the new security agenda.

Increasingly, policy-makers are using military metaphors to describe threats such as AIDS. 'I know of no enemy in war more insidious or vicious than AIDS', Colin Powell told the United Nations in June 2001, '[it is] an enemy that poses a clear and present danger to the world'.[2] The UN Children's Fund (UNICEF) Report the year before had called for the world to go on a 'war footing' to combat the pandemic. Some analysts even describe the HIV virus as a 'phantom warrior'. Protection against AIDS has even become a matter of 'homeland defence'.[3]

Some might object to the redefinition of security itself as emptying the term of any value. They argue, for example, that, compared with those stemming from organised violence, environmental threats are not self-evident or analytically rigorous as concepts. It is all very well to describe the new security agenda but the vagueness of concepts such as 'the war on poverty', or the 'war on AIDS' invites political confusion. The vividness of the war metaphor generates the thought that the challenges and threats are immediate and culture-threatening. Once we cease to be dazzled by the metaphor, we often find less concreteness in the actual analysis of the problems concerned.

And even if we turn to concrete epidemiological threats such as AIDS, not everyone is convinced that this item on the security agenda involves security at all. Or (more to the point) there is no conclusive or widespread agreement on what the security implications of AIDS actually are. One recent US report on the relationship between health and security concluded after eight months of study that there could be no definite conclusion as to whether AIDS constituted a security threat at all.[4]

The use of the word globalisation, of course, can justify anything and everything as a security issue, but even NATO began to acknowledge the realities of the global agenda when its Committee on the Challenges of Modern Society (CCMS) sponsored a pilot study on 'Environment and Security in an International Context'. As its opening statement insisted, with regard to both large-scale and localised environmental problems 'the security dimension is clear'.[5] For security can no longer be tied to states or state sovereignty. Anything that makes the citizen feel insecure (anything that increases personal insecurity) must now be taken into account by governments. At a time when the citizen-soldier has been stood down and conscription abandoned in most armies of the developed world, organised violence is often of much less immediate importance to them than environmental or other concerns.

Since 1993 the United States has had a Deputy Undersecretary of Defense for Environmental Security, and its security agencies (including the State Department and the CIA) are now involved in environmental issues. The US Department of Defense

(DoD) now runs 'outreach' initiatives, and it now holds itself accountable to the concerns of environmental groups. In June 2000 its first-ever Environment, Safety and Occupational Health Report was released. The Strategic Environment R/D Program identified private-sector techniques useful for addressing environmental concerns;[6] one result was the 'green bullet', which aims to minimise the risk of hazardous substances in munitions by making them lead-free. The Ballistic Missile Defence Organisation (not usually noted for its 'green' concerns) even releases reports compiled by its contractors on how their technologies can be used to improve the environment.[7]

The Great Powers may have baulked at intervening in the Great Lakes crisis of 1996 but the Defense Intelligence Agency (DIA) insisted on carrying out a study of the spread of water hyacinth plants in Lake Victoria.[8] And even the weapons the US designs reflect a sensitivity to public concerns: the F-22 fighter uses only one ozone-depleting material. The DoD is the first federal organisation in the United States to meet the Montreal Protocol standards on ozone-depleting emissions.

And it doesn't stop at the environment. As NATO's 1999 Strategic Concept outlines, the future remains hazardous across the spectrum of global concerns:

> *Alliance security must also take account of the global context. Alliance security interests can be affected by other risks of a wider nature, including acts of terrorism, sabotage and organised crime and by the disruption of the flow of vital resources.*[9]

President Clinton's National Security Strategy Report the same year added:

> *Globalisation ... also brings risks ... weapons of mass destruction (WMD), terrorism, drug trafficking and other international crime are global concerns that transcend national borders. Other problems originating overseas – such as resource depletion, rapid population growth, environmental damage, new infectious diseases, pervasive corruption*

> *and uncontrolled refugee migration – have increasingly important implications for American security.*[10]

That was the year that President Clinton personally designated AIDS a national security threat to the United States.

In other words, there is broad agreement that issues such as AIDS and environmental degradation constitute a security threat. And that has less to do with the immediacy of the issues than with the way globalisation has forced us to rethink the concept of security itself. Before looking at this in depth, we should also note that globalisation has done the same in respect of several 'challenges' as diverse as environmental degradation and the HIV-AIDS pandemic. In turn, they have forced governments to rethink the old national security framework in two crucial respects.

i. Some challenges are *unintentional*. The notion of unintended harm – which Marx developed with regard to the market – now encompasses matters such as inequality and migration, which have implications for security that are indirect but significant. Unintended harm is indeed a mark of the global age, and also what it brings with it: uncertainty. As an American general remarked after a military exercise, 'We don't do countries, we do uncertainties'.

ii. Governments now have to accept that both intended and unintended harm are in some degree interconnected. AIDS, for example, raises general public health challenges which are not only an order of magnitude greater than in other periods of history, but which also are shaped by several factors including new technological advances and global trade, both of which interact with health developments. The impact of disease on the environment and biosphere, for example, especially with regard to macro- and micro-ecosystem changes, has led to the emergence of dangerous pathogens – a challenge first highlighted in 1992 at the Rio Conference on Environment and Development.

Similarly, it is no longer possible to separate terrorism from money-laundering. It is impossible to 'wage a war' against one to the exclusion of the other. Such problems are now recognised as the responsibility of the international community, not only individual countries (though individual countries may take the lead in coordinating an international response).

All seven of the challenges I shall identify below are forcing states to look again at what is meant by terms such as 'national security' and even the 'national interest'. No single nation – not even the United States – can tackle these challenges unilaterally, though it may be able to tackle their immediate manifestation (such as the campaign against Al-Qaeda). A globalised age requires global responses as well as coalition politics – the new buzz-word is 'cooperative security.'

Weapons of Mass Destruction (WMD)

Writing in the 1950s the German philosopher Karl Jaspers concluded that the Second World War had produced a single history for the world. Until then, history had been 'a dispersed field of unconnected ventures ... now it is the totality which has become the problem and the task'.[11] Jaspers was writing in the shadow of Hiroshima and Nagasaki. The threat of nuclear war posed a true existential crisis, for it involved the globe for the first time.

Fifty years later Jaspers' fears of global catastrophe seem – on one level – unfounded. One of the great successes of the Cold War era (perhaps even of the Cold War itself) was the absence of weapons proliferation. The superpowers managed not only to avoid using nuclear weapons against each other; they also succeeded in persuading the majority of countries to sign the Nuclear Non-Proliferation Treaty (NPT) and a long list of international agreements intended to prevent the spread of nuclear weapons.

After fifty years, the most striking feature of the nuclear age is that there are so few nuclear states – far fewer, in fact, than predicted by virtually every expert and policy-maker of half a century ago. The experts turned out to be wrong. Of the 31 nations that started down the nuclear path, 22 changed course and renounced the bomb. More importantly, the rate of proliferation has actually declined. After peaking in the 1960s, the number of new nations joining the nuclear club has fallen steadily in each decade, and several of the nations that built or inherited nuclear weapons

– South Africa, Ukraine, Belarus, Kazakhstan – have chosen to renounce them.

Indeed, in the ten years since the end of the Cold War there have been no new nuclear states. India and Pakistan acquired their nuclear-weapons capabilities in the 1970s and 1980s. Iraq and North Korea were near-misses, but in the earlier decades the rate of near-misses was even higher. Indeed, despite all the talk about the dangers of the post-Cold War era, the past ten years have been marked more by renunciation than proliferation. Simply put, the absence of widespread proliferation by states may be one of the great successes of globalisation.[12]

In a global age few responsible states see much advantage in nuclear weapons; indeed the United States and Russia are planning to reduce their stocks quite significantly. But in recent years the WMD issue has acquired much greater global significance because of the very success of non-proliferation. For the more obvious US predominance becomes, the more nuclear weapons may be used for asymmetric purposes. The former Indian Army Chief of Staff, General Sundarji, is reported to have said that the principal lesson of the Gulf War is that, if a state intends to take on the United States, it should first acquire nuclear weapons. And there is now a global trade in nuclear material for states or non-state actors that wish to do precisely that.[13]

And it is this development which justifies Daniel Bell's prediction in 1980 that proliferation would become one of the most likely sources of 'future world disorder'.[14] Today Iraq is rebuilding elements of its WMD infrastructure (probably using the 150-km *Ababil* missile programme to support a longer-range missile effort); Libya has a small *Scud*-B force with a range of 300 km and hopes to acquire longer-range missiles capable of hitting southern Europe; Iran has a delivery system of up to 500 km range and is attempting to acquire fissile material for nuclear weapons. Confronted with this reality, the NATO Strategic Concept of 1999 identified proliferation as a matter of serious concern, which extended its 'action radius' beyond the North Atlantic area.

Proliferation also involves other agents of mass destruction. Chemical weapons, too, are proliferating. China, Cuba, Egypt, Yemen, Iran, Iraq, Israel, Libya, North Korea, Pakistan, Syria and

Taiwan are all suspected of maintaining some chemical stocks. As for biological weapons, some of the chemical-weapon states, including Iraq, Syria, China and North Korea, are known to have operational quantities.

But it is the threat from terrorist movements that is perhaps the most alarming. In the wake of the 11 September World Trade Center attack the World Health Organisation (WHO) felt it 'prudent', not 'alarmist', to bring forward the release of its report that had been due later in the year on preparing for biological or chemical attacks. The organisation thought it important to warn governments of the potential danger. As a spokesman for the WTO was quoted as saying with regard to a terrorist smallpox attack, 'the unthinkable is no longer unthinkable'.[15]

Terrorism

The globalisation of terror has also changed in character as the world moves away from the state-sponsored phenomenon of the 1980s. The statistics tell their own story. Between 1968 and 1989 the rate of terrorist incidents was 1,673 per year. Between 1990 and 1996 there was an increase of 162% on the Cold War years (4,389 a year). The increase would now be closer to 200%, given the escalating number of conflicts since 1996. More alarming is that the new terrorism is primarily conducted against citizens, not governments. Fifty thousand people died in terror attacks between 1990 and 1996 (according to the Rand Corporation), and the main reason people are targeted is that terrorists no longer distinguish between limited and restricted uses of violence.[16]

Globalisation is also producing new, network-centred terrorist organisations. Thus Al-Qaeda is largely a franchising agency that functions through religious internationalism and stateless networks, rather than through the Cold War mechanism of sponsoring states.[17] Paradoxically, while denouncing globalisation, it relies on it to reconstruct a Muslim community beyond national boundaries. Its use of English, the Internet and satellite phones are authentic results of a modern globalised world, even if they serve a movement that is fundamentally in conflict with it. And this is particularly true of radical Islam. Thirty years ago there was not a single religious cult or religious terrorist movement in the world.

As recently as 1980 only two of the world's 64 known terrorist groups were animated by religious belief. Since then Shi'a Muslim groups have accounted for a quarter of all terrorist-related deaths.

As Anatol Lieven contends, the danger to world order comes not from ruling elites integrated into world society but from those numerous social and economic groups who, for whatever reasons (culture, history, geography), are unable to take part in the global success and produce new political pathologies that are profoundly anti-global. 'This is the dark side of the global village – the ability of that village's alienated minorities to hit out at their perceived oppressors over huge distances'.[18] Some of these groups have proud cultural traditions which make it difficult for them to accept second-class status. Others have strong fighting traditions that give them a distinctive edge in certain kinds of warfare. And religion gives them an *expressive* instrument such as suicide bombing.

Indeed, this is one of the paradoxes of globalisation. It creates, when it works, strong opposition to violence between states and even between communities, and so leads to a lower incidence of *instrumental* violence for political ends. But it also engenders the need for *expressive violence* (ritualistic, symbolic and communicative). It engenders terrorism. It creates a sense of powerlessness for those left on a planet where there is no viable alternative to the orthodoxies of the World Bank. It focuses even more attention on America and the 'Americanisation' seeping out of the satellite and cable networks like toxic waste. The expressive violence of the World Trade Center attack had meaning for the victim (anxiety and humiliation) and for the perpetrator (status, prestige and reputation in the Islamic world).[19] And the choice of target, the World Trade Center, a global icon, shows how globalisation gives expressive violence greater symbolic force than ever.

Environment

Equally important, however, are global threats that are not intended either by states or non-state agents. Of these *unintended* challenges to global harmony, perhaps the most important in the public imagination is environmental damage.

It is one of our urban myths that smoke rising from the Amazon forests in 1987 as great swathes of it were cut down could be seen from space along with another work of man, the Great Wall of China. Urban myth or not, the perspective of space was vital in producing a major change of consciousness. Changes *in* consciousness are quite frequent in history; we are often made aware of the external world and respond to it in different ways. We become more sensitive to the suffering of others, or more aware of the existence of issues to which we were previously indifferent. A change *of* consciousness, however, tends to be more profound, for it represents not only a response to the world but challenges many old ideas and beliefs. And it is frequently accompanied by a wish to change the world for the better, in tune with the reinterpretation of reality.

That change of consciousness was first identified by the report *Our Common Future* commissioned by the United Nations in 1983:

> *In the middle of the twentieth century we saw our planet from space for the first time. Historians may eventually find that this vision had a greater impact on thought than did the Copernican revolution of the sixteenth century which upset the human self-image by revealing the Earth is not the centre of the universe.*[20]

Satellite pictures brought home to humanity its fragile position in a limitless universe. They showed the planet in a new light, reformulating in the process the way human beings now see the earth in relation to themselves. It also challenged the narrowness of the old national security framework of thought. Symbolic of this change was the fact that in December 1988 *Time* magazine turned away from its sports heroes and politicians and named the planet as 'Man of the Year', since environmental degradation had now placed it in mortal danger.[21]

Environmental concerns have been the subject of international interest ever since, but at the end of twentieth century they acquired new urgency when the sheer volume of information on environmental crises could no longer be ignored, even by the most sceptical governments. Even if NGOs such as Greenpeace and Friends of the Earth often exaggerate their own case, the rise of these groups in itself is part of a wider sense of global responsibility for the environment and the need to put it on the world's security agenda.

Take the particular issue of climate change. Climate change is occurring at an unprecedented rate because of large quantities of carbon dioxide, methane and other greenhouse gasses being released into the atmosphere on a daily basis. The twentieth century was the warmest century in the past 600 years, and fourteen of the warmest years since the 1860s occurred between 1980 and 1998. Unfortunately, climate change involves the lives of the poorest and most deprived human beings, not (for the moment at least) the most wealthy. If the 'greenhouse effect' and 'global warming' became popular buzz-words in 1988, that was the year that 80% of low-lying Bangladesh was inundated by flood water. Tens of thousands were drowned when a tropical cyclone hit the same area in 1991. If scientists are correct, the greatest threats to humanity from global warming in the short term will come not from millennial climate changes but from regional climatic shifts, which have immediate (and usually adverse) effects on the global population. The tragedy will be even greater as the world's population continues to rise, and marginal environments absorb more and more people.[22]

Governments and international organisations have responded by scrutinising the world through new international organisations. Since the 1970s most of the principal transworld regulating agencies have created special programmes to address environmental issues. They include the OECD Environment Committee (1970), the World Bank Environment Department (1987), the UN Commission on Sustainable Development (1993), and the WTO Committee on Trade and Environment (1995).

At the same time, we must recognise that the environment itself poses a very different challenge from most other security issues, because it has no political or moral standing independent of the interests that political actors invest in it. While states and peoples may feel threatened by environmental change, the environment itself is not a threat. It is not one of those mysterious 'others' against which the Western world is planning to defend itself in the future. It is the environment which is threatened – by human activities and, by extension, by the activities of states.[23] In turn, it is state activity that, through the medium of global warming or climate change, threatens local ecosystems as it also threatens the globe. And this, too, challenges the national security model, for it encourages us to suspect that the state may be the problem, not the solution.

Inequality

Another 'unintended' security threat is global inequality. Nearly thirty years ago the Pearson Commission began its report with the recognition that 'the widening gap between the developed and developing countries has become the central problem of our times'.[24] Over time the gap between the richest fifth of the world's people and the poorest fifth, measured by average national income per head, has more than doubled.[25] Evidence suggests that, as governments have liberalised their economies, almost without exception inequality has increased. As a result the UNDP talks of two globalisations: one for the wealthy, another for the poor.[26]

It is important, however, to distinguish between inequality and poverty. There is now overwhelming evidence that economic growth, which globalisation promotes, leads to reductions in poverty. The number of people in low-income groups has actually fallen from 1.1 billion to 500 million in the past twenty-five years. And for the first time the number of people living in medium- and high-income countries now outstrips the number living in medium- and low-income countries.[27]

But there is no equivalent consensus concerning the role of inequality. Trends, of course, differ from country to country. Tens of millions of Chinese, Malaysians, Brazilians and others have seen their incomes rise substantially. But it is also clear that globalisation has created winners and losers. Concerns are mounting over income inequality and job insecurity in a fast-changing and highly competitive environment which exacerbates a sense of powerlessness and uncertainty.

These trends are reinforcing upward trends in violence. A recent World Bank study of more than 50 countries found a clear relationship between increased income inequality and the murder rate. The UN 'Global Report on Crime and Justice' concludes that socio-economic strains measured in terms of inequality are a major factor in explaining the variation in 'contact crimes' among the countries of the world.[28] And the UN Secretary-General observes: 'Most conflicts take place in poor countries, especially those which are poorly governed or where power and wealth are very unfairly distributed between ethnic or religious groups.'[29] This is one of the most debated questions of all. One study insists that it is not possible to identify a simple and direct connection between global-isation, increases in poverty and armed confrontation. Extreme poverty often induces apathy rather than revolt, and there is no direct evidence to support the proposition that poverty is a prime causal factor in the outbreak of war.[30]

But the prime reason why inequality needs to be addressed is that, if it continues to impoverish already weakened states (Pak-istan, Sri Lanka, Nepal), it will continue to create larger dispos-sessed communities from which terrorist movements may recruit their members in future. The Coalition against terrorism formed after 11 September 2001 was an old-fashioned response to a Clausewitzian threat to security. In the globalised world we live in, the sense of frustration and resentment has to be addressed, and the growth of dispossessed communities stemmed. For both lead the most politically aware or desperate to find in extremist causes and extreme groups some meaning for their lives that they cannot find in the world at large.

Migration

Inequality is important for many reasons, but one of the most important is that it promotes migration. Each year between 2 and 3 million people emigrate. At the beginning of the twenty-first century more than 130 million people were living outside coun-tries of their birth, and that number has been rising by 2% a year. In relative terms the total is a modest 2% of the world's population, but these people are concentrated in just a few regions – and the two most favoured destinations are North America and Western Europe.[31]

Traditionally there have been two kinds of migrants. There are those who have chosen to go abroad to improve their position (or their children's), and those who been forced to flee from political oppression. By the late 1990s conservative estimates of this second group – refugees – put the total number at 30–35 million. The past ten years has seen an unprecedented number on the march as people flee civil wars, ethnic cleansing and mass murder. As the inequalities between the world's richest and poorest countries continue to grow, and as globalisation encourages people to cross frontiers, so refugees continue to flee. With the equivalent of the entire population of the United Kingdom displaced somewhere in the world, what happens to refugees is probably the most important current human-rights issue.

Yet, instead of addressing the problem at source, many governments are retreating behind their defences. In 1999 Canada spent $300 million – ten times what it contributed to the United Nations High Commissioner for Refugees (UNHCR) – on enhancing border controls.[32] Governments are also narrowing the definition of 'refugee' in an attempt to stem the flow into their own countries. At a conference in 1996 nine categories of uprooted people were identified, yet there was no agreement on which of them could claim asylum and which could expect it.[33] All asylum-seekers tend to be lumped together.

Then there are the millions who leave their homes to find work, or improve their economic position. The refugee is a man or woman with a narrower range of choice (real or perceived). And whether the refugee is political or economic is becoming increasingly academic. Even the US Department of Labor concludes that, increasingly, pure refugees and purely economic migrants are 'ideal constructs rarely found in real life'.[34] The traditional distinction between (economic) migrants and (political) refugees is breaking down.

But we also need to see this challenge in the wider context of the post-national distribution of work. The West is expected to export jobs (as well as training opportunities) to low-labour-cost, labour-intensive countries. Work may no longer be tied exclusively to nation states; it may become mobile. Much may depend on whether we find ourselves living in a world in which jobs, rather than people, migrate from region to region and continent to continent. If the division of labour between producers and consumers is being reshaped, then the pressure to emigrate may indeed lessen – the challenge of global migration may even evaporate of its own accord. For the moment, however, this scenario, while undoubtedly attractive, is just that: a scenario.[35]

For Europe, both challenges involve security. It needs immigrants but it also needs to control their influx. The two most pronounced trends in the shaping of its future are the decline in numbers and the ageing of the population. Currently 21% of the population of the EU is over 65. This is expected to rise to 34% by mid-century, meaning that around two-thirds of the population will be not be 'economically active'. As for absolute numbers, the population of Europe in 2000 was 727 million. The UN's 'medium' projection for 2050 is 603 million – a loss of 124 million people or 17%, an unprecedented drop. The 'low' (and probably more likely) projection is 556 million – a loss of 25%.[36]

Since the 1970s most Western countries have returned to the lower birth rates first seen in the 1930s, in almost all cases below the replacement rate. But this time the trend looks likely to continue indefinitely. For there will be no 1950s baby boom. Rather than introducing policies to stimulate the birth rate (the preference of the 1930s), governments are introducing policies that encourage immigration. Advocates of immigration, of course, point out that its adds new perspectives, diversity and richness to a nation's cultural and economic life: it is regenerative. The case has been persuasively made that the new entrepreneurs of an increasingly knowledge-based economy gravitate towards centres of multicultural vitality. But the critics are also right to point out that it also brings social dislocation and community tension. Any population with sub-replacement fertility (the current UK and German positions) that attempts to maintain a given population size through immigration would acquire a population of predominantly, eventually entirely, immigrant origin. Populations can only adopt this solution to stabilise numbers at the risk of their original identity.

The security dimension of the challenge is twofold. First, governments will have to reassure the native populations that immigration is necessary to sustain economic growth and standards of living. Second, they can only do this if immigration is managed and controlled so that it does not fuel support for far-right or neo-fascist movements.

There is another factor, as well, which may alarm public opinion in Europe even further. The majority of immigrants will be Muslim. A demographic explosion in North Africa leading to a massive influx would have a catastrophic impact on political and social stability. In Morocco high unemployment and minimal prospects for upward mobility have prompted a crisis of confidence in the future; according to a 1998 survey nearly 90% of Moroccans in their twenties wanted to leave the country. As the former Spanish Foreign Minister, Javier Solana, once confessed, the region already has 'all the ingredients for the conflict between Islam and Europe that has made up so much of the unhappy history of the Mediterranean'.[37] The western Mediterranean is a potential 'interface' between two historically antagonistic cultures that may well find themselves in conflict again in the future.

Organised Crime

One security challenge which owes almost everything to globalisation is that of organised crime, which has now moved away from the traditional clan-based and localised models, such as the Jamaican Yardies and the Sicilian mafia, to transnational networks that are structured like international business. As crime becomes more business-like it becomes more difficult to detect, for criminal groups make full use of global technologies, including the Internet and e-commerce.

In 1986 NSC Directive 221 for the first time declared drug-trafficking a threat to national security. President Clinton's Presidential Decision Directive 42 extended the definition to global organised crime as a whole. Crime is now, in the words of one analyst 'an imminent threat to the nation state'.[38] Yet in dealing with crime the line between foreign and domestic policies has become increasingly blurred. National approaches have been centred on two areas, 'defence and security' and 'public safety'. There is now an urgent need to address the two concepts together.

Particularly worrying is the level of criminal global penetration and the threat it poses to legitimate economic development. For the world's drug syndicates cooperate extensively and intensively to achieve economies of scale and wide margins of profit. It is estimated that the narcotics trade alone represents 10% of the world's money in circulation at any one time. The leading Colombian banks now have to track the dealing price of cocaine on the streets of New York because of its impact on the local exchange rates: a scarcity of cocaine, hence a higher price, in New York means a scarcity of dollars in Colombia itself. The attempt by law-enforcement officers to halt the shipment of illegal proceeds of the drug trade seems futile in the face of such stark laws of supply and demand.

Not surprisingly, organised crime has been called the shadowy sign of globalisation.[39] Indeed, it can be seen as part of a larger phenomenon: the rise of a large but little-discussed illicit global economy which finances an uncontrolled arms trade, money-laundering, a narcotics trade worth $500 billion per annum, smuggling illegal immigrants, trafficking in endangered species, dumping of toxic waste, and promoting prostitution and child labour.[40]

The activities of organised crime should be of concern to the security community because they undermine global order. International crime has played a major role, for example, in the proliferation of small arms: the availability of illegal weapons has destabilised local or regional orders and helped fuel ethnic conflicts from Africa to the Balkans. In these conflicts there is strong evidence of a 'floating market'. As demand is satisfied in one part of the region, dealers look to developing new customers, while falling prices allow more actors to enter the market.[41] Elsewhere – in Kosovo – NATO has had to confront the close working relationship between elements of the KLA and the Albanian mafia. The KLA allowed the movement of heroin across its territory in return for money and weapons; the Albanian drug gangs benefited by access to relatively secure drug routes and a degree of legitimation from within their own expatriate community as 'quartermasters' of the war.[42]

In an attempt to counteract the problem there have been a plethora of regional and sub-regional organisations which include the UN Programme for Combating and Preventing Illicit Arms Trafficking, the EU pre-accession pact on organised crime, and the South-eastern Europe Cooperation Initiative (SECI) for combating cross-border crime. Regrettably, many of these initiatives have yet to be fully implemented, while others have suffered from lack of support. The OECD's attempts to address arm-trafficking suffered when its database on international cooperation between agencies was shut down for lack of funds.

HIV-AIDS

Of all the new security challenges that globalisation has thrown up none is more grim than that of HIV-AIDS. At the end of 2000, 36 million people were living with HIV or full-blown AIDS; 5.3 million were infected for the first time, and 3 million died (on any given day, the number of people dying of AIDS-related illnesses is double the number of the victims of the attack on the World Trade Center). Seventy percent of them are to be found in sub-Saharan Africa, where more than 5 million became newly infected in 1999 alone. The spread of the pandemic has multiple consequences for development. It robs countries of people in their prime and leaves children uncared for. Within a decade nearly a third of the total productive population of Southern Africa will die or fall seriously ill from HIV-AIDS and its related epidemics such as malaria, tuberculosis and dysentery, giving rise to the prospect of failed regions as well as failed states.[43]

The belief that AIDS represents a global crisis has gained momentum in recent years. As a result AIDS was the first health issue ever to be addressed by the UN Security Council, which admitted that 'post-Cold War security is about more than guns and bombs and the balance of power'.[44] Adding its own contribution, the US National Intelligence Council (NIC) produced a Global Infectious Diseases Report the same month which identified the spread of AIDS as a threat to its own national security. And as the year came to a close the US National Security Strategy for a Global Age acknowledged that 'interdependence has caused disease and health risks around the world to become matters of both US national and international security'.[45]

There is certainly no consensus on how this may happen. Some analysts identify the global challenge as failed regions (not merely failed states). The US National Foreign Intelligence Board Report *Global Trends 2015* believes AIDS will threaten the successful peaceful transition to democracy in many countries, especially in Africa and Asia. It will undermine civil society and fuel the competition for scarce resources.[46] The US also has solid, old-fashioned security interests in combating AIDS in Africa. South Africa has been defined as a 'pivotal state,' whose future will determine stability or instability in the whole region for years to come.

In more concrete terms, the future of peacekeeping is also questioned. UN Resolution 1308, adopted in July 2000, underscores the need for a UN Department of Peacekeeping Operations to incorporate HIV/AIDS-prevention awareness skills and advice in its training for peacekeeping operations. The problem for the military is that it is the highest risk group. Peacetime sexually transmitted infections in both developed and developing countries are apparently between two and five times higher in the military than civilian levels; during wartime the risk for the military is up to 100 times higher. UN missions are especially at risk.[47] Stationed for extended periods in stressful, alien environments, removed from families and familiar culture, soldiers tend to resort to sex workers more than most. And, to make matters worse, the possibility of infection cuts both ways. Peacekeeping can spread the virus among the host population when soldiers arrive back from their missions abroad. The estimated HIV prevalence rate is as high as 20% in the armed forces of Nigeria (one of the principal peacekeeping nations), and India – another – is likely to have the highest AIDS rate in the world within a decade.[48]

This is yet another illustration of how globalisation (belatedly to be sure) is forcing itself into the consciousness of the international community. But the AIDS debate is interesting for another reason which touches upon all the threats just discussed. If the military metaphor is common in the new security discourse, there is little agreement about where the battle lines are drawn: in the case of HIV, is the war against the virus or against the people who have it? In the international realm, will this lead to countries to write off Africa or the countries most at risk? AIDS has already become a determinant of the African condition. For many it is another feature of what *The Economist* calls 'the hopeless continent'.

In the end AIDS is a metaphor – and that's where the danger lies. We talk of viruses and long incubation periods as more dangerous than the illness itself. HIV is a 'stealth' virus, because you can live with it for years without knowing you have contracted it. Like the disease, the new security challenges encourage us to think of security not so much in terms of what is but of what may yet become. Thus, instead of trying to confront a danger, we try to confront dangerousness – an idea which means that the threat must be considered by society at the level of its potentiality, not its immediate consequences. [49] It is an excellent example of our risk age and what it gives rise to: the emergence of risk communities.

Rethinking Security in a Globalised Age

The world market, Tony Blair argued twenty-two days into the Kosovo War, was only 'the most obvious' case of globalisation. Globalisation was not a matter of economic integration alone. When Blair told his audience in Chicago 'we are all internationalists now', he did not mean that internationalism was an ideological choice as it had been in the past. Internationalism was now the foundation of the international community, and thus a central condition for conducting politics.

> *Today the impulse towards interdependence is immeasurably greater. We are witnessing the beginnings of a new doctrine of international community. By this I mean the explicit recognition that today more than ever before we are mutually dependent, that national interest is to a significant extent governed by international collaboration and that we need a clear and coherent debate as to the direction this doctrine takes us in each field of international endeavour. Just as within domestic politics, the notion of community – the belief that partnership and cooperation are essential to advance self-interest – is coming into its own, so it needs to find its international echo.*[50]

An echo of such thinking can be seen in the three different ways in which we are beginning to look at security.

Human Security

The reason so much importance is attached to AIDS, for example, is because it is one of those issues that falls under the remit of 'human security'. This notion was initially advanced by the UNDP in its 1994 *Human Development Report*, which, in turn, sought to put the individual, not the state, at the centre of the picture, and to focus on his or her interests at the expense of the traditional state-centric approach. The term 'human security' is now used by a growing number of security experts to stress that in a global age the life of the individual, family and community are all important. Hunger, safety and the security of the environment have all moved centre stage. 'Human security' has even been officially adopted by Japan, Norway and Canada. Other governments are likely to follow suit.

To be global is to go beyond the national security framework. There is a domestic parallel here, the attempt by governments since the 1960s to redress the incivility still to be found in social life. At home this has encompassed such diverse themes as the campaign against rape in marriage, as well as violence against children, together with the violence that is still often concealed in institutions such as prisons and schools. What those campaigns have revealed is the extent to which civil societies are plagued by endemic sources of incivility – so much so that we might conclude that incivility, if not one of its defining conditions, is a chronic feature of civil society itself.

The phenomenon can be taken as evidence of 'social fatigue'.[51] The majority of child-abusers, for example, tend to be found within the home. In the United States 20 children in every 100,000 die in acts of violence, and 60% of those charged with murder are usually parents of the child. Often they are seen, or see themselves, as victims of a civil society that does not work for them. They find themselves trapped within its 'high-tension zones'. Usually disguised, violence erupts from time to time whenever a person's inability to cope with the demands of social life is combined with a chronic insecurity that arises from (say) a break in regular patterns of employment.

On the international level this has led to the rise of what Robertson calls a global consciousness which focuses not on the traditional security concerns but the 'hidden' factors of incivility in warfare, such as the use of land-mines. The ban on land-mines imposed by the Ottawa Convention (1997) illustrates the concept of 'human security' at work. For the convention became the first legally binding disarmament instrument to ban a widely deployed weapon of war as well as the quickest major international agreement to come into force. In response, two years later the final operational anti-personnel landmine HB876, a submunition of the RAF's JP233 airfield-denial weapon, was dismantled.

As Canada's Foreign Minister Lloyd Axworthy pointed out when the Convention was being debated, the basic unit of security is no longer the state but human need. In May 1998 Canada joined Norway in launching a joint initiative on human security, working together on other issues – such as that of child soldiers, of whom there are now more than 300,000 in the world. The land-mines campaign itself was framed through the human-security lens and based on the premise that the lives of civilians must take precedence even over national security interests. It was hailed at the time as an example of the new partnership between states, international organisations and NGOs. As the UN Deputy Secretary General Louise Frechette remarked at the time, in working with non-government organisations in this field, governments now recognise the latter as 'the global conscience'.[52]

Preventive Defence

The second way in which globalisation has forced governments to reconceptualise security stems from the first. Human security requires *preventive* action to reduce the risk to human safety and human lives. It stresses the importance of acting early, because it is more humane and also more effective.

Two former DoD officials, Ashton Carter and William Perry, have produced a defence strategy that concentrates on dangers that, if mismanaged, may have the potential to grow into 'A-list' threats such as nuclear proliferation and catastrophic terrorism. As the authors acknowledge, preventive defence is fundamentally different from deterrence, for it draws on all the instruments of foreign policy: political, economic and military. When they were in government Ashton and Perry had made a start in implementing that policy. It is embodied in the 1997 Quadrennial Defence Review, which clearly states that 'shaping the international environment' is now one of America's principal military missions.[53]

As John Steinbrunner adds, 'one of the most fundamental implications of globalisation is the shift in the balance of reliance in security policy from deterrence to reassurance and from active confrontation to cooperative agreement'.[54] He goes on to point out that one of the major implications of this shift is that the emerging problems of security are no longer primarily concerned with the defence of territory, as in the past, but with the promotion and defence of legal norms. Virtually every state in the world, for example, now accepts the concept of human rights, and to that extent is now legally accountable for any abuses. A substantial number of states have signed up to the UN Conventions on Economic, Social and Political Rights. Every member state of the Council of Europe has ratified the European Convention for the Protection of Human Rights. Seventeen states of the Western hemisphere now adhere to the American Convention on Human Rights. And these conventions have to be enforced. They create the legal basis for humanitarian intervention and require governments to be interested in the actions of other governments or states. The international community is now responsible for policing legal regimes, treaties, conventions and protocols involving issues as diverse as weapons proliferation, arms control, human rights and humanitarian and environmental law.

Public–Private–Voluntary Partnership

The land-mines issue also illustrates the growth of transnational 'risk communities', which coalesce around common concerns. It brought together over 1,300 diverse groups, with interests covering human rights, children, peace, disability, environmental, arms control and women's groups, in 75 different countries. In 1999 the UN Deputy Secretary General claimed that the emergence of networks such as the International Campaign to Ban Landmines

(ICBLM) was as important as the rise of the nation state in earlier centuries.[55] And, even if there may be an element of hyperbole in this claim, Kofi Anan was still right to see the Ottawa Convention as the decision of governments taken 'under the influence of NGO advocacy'.[56]

We must be careful, of course, not to exaggerate their role. For states are still central. Without them international conventions would not be signed or have any force at all, but now the 'imagined community' of the nation is being forced to share its political space with other imagined communities, especially that of global civil society. In the case of the World Bank, the rate of NGO involvement rose from 6% in 1988 to 30% in the 1990s. UNHCR has relations with over 500 NGOs whom it describes as 'partners in action'. Indeed, without NGO pressure the United Nations would never have set up its Human Rights Commission.

NGOs' participation in the United Nations Framework Convention on Climate Change (UNFCC) has increased substantially. Since its inception in 1992 the number of organisations accredited as observers has risen from 191 (1995) to 530 (2000).[57] In the humanitarian field, too, the US government is also working increasingly with NGOs. The DoD now sponsors a Center of Excellence in Disaster Management and Humanitarian Assistance affiliated with the US Pacific Command. Another was established in 1999 to work with the US Southern Command. Both centres facilitate the flow of information among international organisations, NGOs and the military and provide the military with a source of expertise in humanitarian assistance.[58]

And Western governments are not only working with the voluntary sector, they are also contracting out to it. Private agencies are already implementing public policy. In the words of the former US Secretary of State Madeleine Albright, the willingness of governments to work with them now represents a 'force multiplier'.[59] 'Interaction', a coalition of 160 US private relief and refugee agencies, has a Field Cooperation Protocol which emphasises the need for NGO–military cooperation. In the case of the Kosovo war, a month before the outbreak of hostilities the United States government contracted out to a private security company, Dyncorp, its role in the OSCE Observer mission, largely to avoid putting its own military personnel at risk. The process was carried to its logical conclusion when the war began. Unwilling to drop food parcels to refugees because of the operational risks to its pilots, the US contracted out the mission instead to a consortium of NGOs called the International Rescue Committee.

Chapter 4

The Risk Community

This brings me to another way in which globalisation has reshaped the way governments think about security: the distribution of risk. Governments are increasingly sharing risks with the private and voluntary sectors. The private–voluntary–public partnership to which politicians increasingly refer is their way of ensuring that criticism of operations or initiatives is shared across a spectrum of opinion. It is a typical response of a risk society.

Seeking a general explanation for why our societies are more anxious about risks than ever is a matter that has engaged sociologists like Ulrich Beck, Anthony Giddens and other writers for many years. All of them are agreed that it is common to what they call 'second modernity', 'late modernity', or the 'post-modern age'. Perhaps, the last expression is the best – or at least one that has entered general currency. Speaking at the Davos World Economic Forum in 1992 Vaclav Havel remarked that sooner or later 'politics will be faced with the task of finding a new, post-modern face'.[1] And the same might be said of security.

Entering into the debate on post-modernity is well beyond the scope of this Paper, but, if we seek a definition of the term, we might invoke Baudelaire, who was not only the first writer to coin the term 'modernity' but also the first to describe 'progress' as 'the great modern idea'.[2] Today we are more sober about both progress and the future. For, although we still accept that things may progress, we now recognise there is a price to be paid. We are now increasingly wary of the consequences of our own actions, and can no longer take progress on trust. Post-modernity has been defined as a 'more modest modernity', a sign of modernity coming to terms with its own limits.[3] And one of those limits is the *global* consequences of our actions, initiatives and projects. In that sense, if in no other, it makes sense to talk of globalisation as a historical era. For the post-modern condition is one we all experience in a mode that is more than ever defined by risk: by the cluster of risks, insecurities and control problems that have played a crucial role in shaping our changing response to the world. Concern about risk is no longer a peripheral matter; it is built into the environment, culture and the everyday routines that guide our lives. In this sense we live in a 'risk age'. Risk has become a way of thinking about one's moment in history; it is not only inherent in the moment itself.

It remains to ask: when did the risk community first emerge? For Mary Douglas, the current concern with risk is a product of globalisation and what it brings – a sense of vulnerability in being part of a world system. For her, this first manifested itself in the late 1950s, which saw a debate about 'le défi Américain': the fear that American multinational corporations were about to dispossess Europe of its economic sovereignty.[4] For Ulrich Beck, the key period was the 1970s, which saw the rise of chemical hazards from the new industries and technologies which were truly global in their impact on the environment.[5] Indeed the hidden costs of technology can be devastating. Once (in the 1950s) believed to offer a limitless source of energy, nuclear power has never recovered from the bad press of Chernobyl and Three Mile Island. Some harm can be hidden for decades: chlorofluorocarbons (CFCs), invented in 1928, were only proved conclusively to be harmful to the ozone layer fifty years later – and they are still used in many countries and will not be phased out until 2010. And still the debate continues. Genetically modified plants are suspected of creating super-weeds and introducing new sources of allergens. Information and communications technology facilitates international crime, supports the drug network, and assists the dissemination of child pornography. Technological change, like all change, poses risks – as shown by the industrial disaster in Bhopal, the nuclear disaster in Chernobyl, the birth defects from Thalidomide, the depletion of the ozone layer by CFCs. The more novel and fundamental the change, the less is known about its potential consequences and hidden costs. Hence a general mistrust of scientists, private corporations and governments – indeed, of the whole technology establishment.

Beck recognises that all societies, whether pre-modern, modern or late modern, face dangers, but he reserves the right to use the term 'risk society' of the third era, our own. For today risk has changed everything, especially the way we conceive security. What is interesting is the way in which this knowledge has worked into the mindset of all communities, including the security world. We talk of 'the war on AIDS' and 'the war on want' and 'the war against crime'. The metaphors, in turn, invest the risks with even more apocalyptic overtones and even greater global resonance. Global risks make us insecure because they have become endless, too large and too apocalyptic to be contained within regimes or new world orders. The anti-globalisers on the US right may fear the rise of a New World Order (NWO) conspiracy, but the so-called conspirators (including their own government) do not feel in charge. Instead they confront what President Clinton called 'a world in which risk is endless'.[6]

Risks as Global

It is a commonplace belief of our times that we think we are subject to risks that are potentially more catastrophic because they are global. As Ernest Gellner explained, risk became central in our thinking and behaviour once we entered a global society. For globalisation has drawn us out of our self-contained national or local communities into a larger world that offers none of the old protections. It is impossible to offer private insurance against many, if not most, of the risks we now face; the market sets us free of the local, but leaves us exposed to the global.[7]

And global risks cannot be delimited *spatially*. Indeed, they are becoming more difficult to manage because of their non-localised nature. In the past, risks were largely perceptible. People could see unsanitary conditions for themselves, and localised areas where they were at risk; they could choose, if they wished, to avoid them. Today the risks are global, implicit in post-industrialisation and in the main unseen. And they are no longer delimited even by *time*. Chernobyl and the hazard of nuclear contamination, like that of the pollution of rivers and the long-term dangers of toxic waste, mean that the consequences of such hazards are not always immediate. One of the most poignant covers of *Time* was of Gulf War veterans' children who had suffered genetic defects as a result of their fathers' possible exposure to chemical agents on the battlefield. The article accompanying the photographs was called, 'The Tiny Victims of Desert Storm'.[8] And that is the source of many of our anxieties: in future, soldiers may survive a campaign, but their children may not.

So, when we conceptualise security we do so in terms of risk itself. The language of danger has now turned into the language of risk. Globalisation has ensured that the risk society, broadly speaking, is a society organised in a significant way around the concept of risk. Risk increasingly determines the discourse of security.

Policing Risks

Every society that has faced dangers has evolved security strategies to deal with them. But the difference today is that the risks, being global, cannot be calculated with any degree of certainty. And, being global, they cannot be *insured* against. If for no other reason than symbolism, the idea of private insurance is an interesting one, for it is impossible to privately insure oneself against nuclear disaster, climate change and its consequences, or the Asian financial crisis. Only the most *un*likely risks, such as alien abduction, are now covered by the insurance business, although so far in only one state – Florida.

In a way, the situation is analogous to the fate of the welfare state in Western Europe. As Francois Ewald argues, the welfare state can be seen as an attempt to provide security for a people who demanded it after the trauma of the Second World War. The provision of services such as free health care, the creation of insurance schemes and the regulation of the economy were all undertaken to create security, or at least a sense of it. The need for a new social contract, a lesson learned from the inter-class conflicts that had weakened Europe's democracies in the run-up to the war, accounted to some extent for a form of capitalism that is still intrinsically different from the classical model.[9]

Germany, for example, has a socially financed apprenticeship scheme and social welfare policies that are not usually seen as a necessary part of the market-economy mechanism. In the German model (unlike the American) a centralised level of control is considered preferable to decentralised power. Central controls are deemed necessary to prevent irresponsible fiscal policies likely to encourage high interest rates, high inflation and thus greater insecurity. Of course, as the twenty-first century opens, the social-market model faces an increasing challenge. As labour costs have risen, the European economy has become less competitive.

What is true at the domestic level is also true at the international. The new security regimes set up after the war, such as NATO and the Marshall Plan, were intended to secure for the peoples of the 'free world' the four freedoms promised by Roosevelt in the 1940s: freedom from want, freedom from fear, freedom of worship and freedom of speech. Of the four, the first two – equating to freedom from insecurity – were judged the most important. Just as the welfare model is now under threat from the forces of globalisation, which dictate that economies be as competitive as possible in order to survive, so the old security regimes like the ABM Treaty are under threat too. The collapse of concepts such as the New International Economic Order in the 1980s and the New World Order in the 1990s merely confirms an innate scepticism that risks can be eliminated or even significantly reduced. Instead, all we can do is manage them.

We no longer seek to insure against them by constructing new world orders or putting together new security systems, as we did in the past. Instead we have a risk-management ethos, which has emerged in response to the greater insecurity that seems to stem from globalisation. Fukuyama, the erstwhile prophet of *The End of History* now writes of *The Great Disruption* that accompanies the risk culture. And the management of risk now operates at two levels (both of which accompany a decline in the belief that the international community – or even the world's last remaining superpower – can deal with the root causes of insecurity, as the founding fathers of the Western Alliance once believed). One is surveillance: 'global neighbourhood watch' programmes, the constant war to minimise opportunities for offending – the practical, low-visibility operations that excite little public interest or debate. The second is the new 'panics', like the war against terrorism, the dramatic campaigns against new criminal scourges, and public demands for harsher punishment. Both responses to risk emphasise control – which, of course, is elusive, since there can be no termination of terrorism, or pandemics or the trade in narcotics.

The principle military rationale is now 'preventive defence' against a myriad of dangers, most of them abstract and undefined. 'There is a universe of potentials we have to deal with', declared the US Homeland Security Chief, Tom Ridge, after the World Trade Center attack.[10] 'When I was coming up', claimed George W Bush on the campaign trail in 2000, 'it was a dangerous world and we knew exactly who they were. It was us versus them and it was clear who them was – Today, we're not so sure who the they are but we know they're there'.[11] In his tortured syntax, Bush expresses the abiding reality of the hour. Compare this with his father's speech on the campaign trail in 1988, when he promised the American people that the Strategic Defense Initiative (SDI) would offer them 'an exit from history'. In those (now remote) days, it seemed possible to offer people a permanent solution to the problem of nuclear war. Today there are no solutions, only risk-management strategies. What George Bush offered in 1991, a 'new world order', is no longer on anyone's lips.

Instead of managing security, we manage insecurity (nuclear proliferation, terrorism, etc.) through *pre-emptive* action if possible. For not acting is often seen as an even more unacceptable risk. *Operation Essential Harvest* in Macedonia was justified by the NATO Secretary General in precisely these terms: 'there are risks involved, but the risks of not sending the troops are far higher'.[12] In his official statement on the commencement of military operations in Afghanistan in October 2001 Blair acknowledged 'the dangers in acting', but insisted that the 'dangers of not acting [were] much higher'.[13]

In this world of uncertainties and risks the only option open to governments is to police the world. And in a globalised age we see the emergence of a new concept of policing, which takes its cue from the domestic model, where people have moved from 'community policing' to 'policing communities of risk'. In many Western societies 'disciplinary' techniques are no longer aimed at altering individual behaviour. Policing is no longer corrective or transformative. We have replaced the old moral and clinical description of criminals with a risk one: cost. There is no longer concern to treat individual offenders or even rehabilitate them; instead the focus is on classifying groups according to the dangers they pose to society and managing them accordingly. The target group is no longer the criminal but the community of potential victims. Hence the interest in 'zero-tolerance' policing, 'moving on' criminals or potential criminals, and the constant surveillance of those potential criminals, individuals or groups, in order to make policing more effective.[14]

If constant surveillance has become the vehicle of risk-management at home, it is also the vehicle of global management. Where rogue states (rather than situations) are identified, they are designated members of 'risk groups' and are subject to constant surveillance by satellite. Variously described as 'rogues', 'pariahs', 'outlaws' and most recently 'states of concern' they are all part of the new strategic lexicon. Iraq heads the list, but others are not far behind.[15] The surveillance of northern Iraq is aptly named 'Operation Northern Watch'.

Air power is the preferred medium by which risks are policed. It began with the no-fly zones in northern Iraq above the 36th parallel, and in southern Iraq below the 33rd. Both were established after the 1991 war, to protect the Marsh Arabs and Shi'i Muslims in the south and the Kurds in the north from Iraqi reprisals after uprisings in both areas of the country had failed to unseat Saddam Hussein. No-fly zones are justified by UN Security Council Resolution 688 (5 April 1991), which deems the Iraqi repression of these minorities 'a threat to international security'. In the course of time the air missions have become less an instrument for protecting the Kurds (they have little impact on Iraqi actions on the ground) and more a means of constraining Saddam Hussein's freedom of action. By the end of the 1990s the US and Britain had launched 200,000 air sorties in all; by then the policing had become permanent (when George W Bush sanctioned the first air strike of his presidency in February 2001 he described the mission as 'routine').[16]

When we do turn to the military option, we do so to reduce the opportunities for bad behaviour, to prevent them from posing an even greater risk in the future. The style is one of containment, confinement and dissuasion. And since there is no end to the problem (as opposed to the enemies) we face, since there is no end in sight to nuclear proliferation, managing insecurity will probably continue well into the future. It is the only insurance we have. But we should also recognise that all risk-management strategies have hidden costs. Sanctions against Iraq have led to enormous human suffering. As a 1999 UN report stresses, 'the gravity of the humanitarian situation of the Iraqi people is indisputable and cannot be overstated'; the country has experienced 'a shift from relative affluence to massive poverty'.[17] In Serbia the percentage of the population living in poverty after the Kosovo War rose from 33% to 63%, and 250,000 Serbs lost their jobs as a result of the bombing. Moreover, to keep Milosevic on the defensive, the West insisted on a ban on reconstruction aid and for the first time put pressure on the UNHCR and the International Committee of the Red Cross to reduce their existing programmes to Serbia.

So, the 'war' against terrorism, like those against crime and the many other 'uncertainties' and challenges that form the West's security agenda, are often invisible in terms of their consequences for people on the ground. And this raises an awkward question. War is largely transparent; crisis management is not. War involves victims; crisis management does too, but its victims do not always appear on the TV screens or even enter the public consciousness. In its distaste for 'war' and its preference for engaging in 'risk-management strategies', is the West becoming more ruthless and aggressive? War, writes Michael Mandelbaum, once the policy of the strong is now the policy of the weak. 'Wars', however, are purely the policy of the strong, and a little more honesty and self-awareness might make Western management of global risks seem to the rest of the world less arrogant or morally disengaged.

Chapter 5

NATO and the Challenge of Globalisation

As a community, the Western world has the most to defend. NATO still represents the rich world. And that world at the beginning of the twenty-first century is not all that different from what it was at the beginning of the twentieth: 54% of world production is accounted for by the industrial countries (excluding the newly industrialised Asian economies), and an even larger share (68%) of world trade. It is true that some of the total is accounted for by Japan, but the West still trades overwhelmingly with itself. Approximately 60% of North American and as much as 84% of West European trade flows are accounted for from within the Alliance. Indeed, half of all world trade is now conducted between NATO nationals.[1]

As Linda Weiss also points out, as of 1991, 81% of the world stock of foreign direct investment was also located in high-wage northern countries: the United States, followed by the United Kingdom, Germany and Canada. Instead of declining, the concentration of investment in these countries has risen significantly since 1967. As a result, NATO countries can be said to have the most important 'investment' in globalisation.[2] They are the most globalised countries in the world as well as the most at risk from the threats that globalisation raises.

In the remainder of this Paper I am going to look at the extent to which transnationalism has changed NATO's security agenda and the context in which decisions are made. The first reference to the term was made in the aftermath of the First World War, by

Norman Angel in his book *The Fruits of Victory* (1921), when he identified an international, or more correctly, a 'transnational economy'. In the late 1960s Kenneth Galbraith identified – in addition to the ethnocentric, polycentric and geocentric types of multinational company – a fourth type: the transnational, with international stock ownership. Since then the term has come to be used of the growing number of interactions that sustain world politics and that unfold without the direct involvement of nations or states.[3]

After discussing the transnational challenges to NATO, I will then look at the extent to which the Alliance is no longer a 'security community' but a *risk community*, an institution more suited to a post-Cold War age. I will conclude by looking at the Alliance's defence of what is called 'the doctrine of international community' and the three global dialectics I identified in the introduction to this Paper, all of which NATO will have to address if it is to remain a viable organisation.

The Challenge of Transnationalism

Many of the forces underlying the transnational character of the international system are largely anonymous and therefore difficult to identify, but James Rosenau has distinguished five to which nation states the world over are increasingly being forced to respond.[4]

- *Transnational organisations.* For the first time NGOs have moved from the spectators' gallery to the decision-making table. They have forced the World Bank to review its funding strategy; helped to create the post of UN High Commissioner for Human Rights and derailed the World Trade Organisation (WTO) talks in Seattle. At the World Economic Forum in Davos in January 2001 representatives from 15 NGOs were invited for the first time to take part in the debates on globalisation.
- *Transnational politics.* Ethnic conflicts, the narcotics trade, and even AIDS, are increasingly determining the political agenda.
- *Transnational events* such as the publication of a novel (Rushdie's *Satanic Verses*) can have an impact on a diverse range of countries, separated by geography but brought together by cable networks such as Al-Jazeera and CNN.

- *Transnational communities* can develop around a religion (Islam), or lifestyles and deeply held belief systems (environmentalism), which challenge the integrity or authority of nation states.
- *Transnational structures* such as banks, financial flows or new technologies (Internet) create new contexts of action and provoke crises across large distances.

These five transnational forces can be said to have sometimes challenged or even undermined the sovereignty of the nation state. And NATO, as an alliance of nation states, has experienced each of them at one time or another.

Transnational organisations, in the form of aid agencies and human-rights activists, increasingly determine where and why the Alliance acts. Their role was a not unimportant element in the deteriorating relationship between the United States and Europe over Bosnia in the early 1990s. What states once considered central to their rationale, the use of force, is subject these days (to quote a British General) 'to what the market will allow'.[5] What the 'market' (public opinion) expects should be done is also important (it is called 'public determinism'). It is this development which explains NATO's evolution from a collective defence alliance into a collective security alliance which has gone into the business of conducting humanitarian wars.

NGOs have forced NATO to address new problems. Hence the de-mining issue led to the Global Humanitarian De-mining Initiative launched in the Euro-Atlantic Partnership Council (EAPC). And the influence is not all one way. As Madeleine Albright wrote after the Kosovo War, 'by melding the capabilities of the military and Non Government Organisations and private voluntary organisations you have developed a force multiplier.'[6] The West tends, in fact, to take NGOs for granted – it is worth remembering that, as of 1995, all but 15% of all international NGOs were Western – and one of the NGOs' concerns is the extent to which they are becoming identified with the Alliance, and what this means for their perceived impartiality. During the Kosovo war seven leading French NGOs wrote an open letter in *Le Monde* regretting the extent to which they had become identified with NATO's military action. Regrettable or not, both sides have to share the same humanitarian space; both will have to manage relations with each other more effectively in future.

Transnational problems, by contrast, were the principle motivation for NATO's air war against Milosevic. Containing the mass migration of peoples is one of the collective security problems of the day, and one way of confronting the problem head on is to go to source: to prevent or punish ethnic cleansing. Environmental fallout is another problem that spans frontiers and intermeshes governments in political disputes. Before the signing of the Dayton Accord, the mining of the hydro-electric Bijelo Polje power station in Mostar and Serb forces' systematic shelling of chemical plants in Tuzla in the winter of 1993–4 aroused particular concern amongst environmental groups in Europe. Several years later, and halfway through the air war in Kosovo, NATO became aware of growing NGO concern at the environmental damage occasioned by its own air strikes. Had the air campaign continued much longer it might have been forced to reconsider its target set.

The Alliance was left in no doubt either of the importance of *transnational events* when it bombed the Chinese Embassy in Belgrade. The UN neither devolved responsibility in the war to NATO nor subcontracted to it, as it had in Bosnia, but the tacit acquiescence of two of its permanent members, China and Russia, was vital to the final settlement. The problem is that an event in Europe can have dramatic consequences 8,000 miles away. This was the case in China, where the embassy bombing brought out the largest street crowds seen since the 4 May Movement in 1919. Not all the protests were orchestrated by the government: many were spontaneous, as world opinion became increasingly disturbed by what it considered to be evidence of unilateralism on the part of the United States. The problem with transnational events is that the West makes more history than anyone else simply by virtue of being increasingly transparent: the world is watching it much more than it is watching the world.

The rise of *transnational communities* has also been a vital element in NATO's calculations about its future role. The nation may still be a person's primary reference point, but nationalism, in that sense, is far less important than at any time since the experience of nation-building. States and nations are becoming delinked.

Nations now are becoming more than, but also less than, nation states. Movements like 'The Islamic Nation' transcend boundaries. Identities are escaping the confines or framework of the nation-state structure into a cultural space defined in terms of globality rather than territory.

Indeed, one of the chief features of European politics is the growth of bicultural partnerships. Europe is in the process of becoming a multi-cultural society, with a 'transcultural' generation that will have affinities with two cultures, not one. Muslims already account for 10% of the European Union's labour force, and Islam is by far its fastest-growing religion. Many Muslims identify with Islam more than their own nation states; others find a serious conflict between the two when wars involve the Muslim world. Such a conflict of identities was a feature of the almost unanimous hostility among Muslim citizens in Europe to the war against the Taliban and bin Laden.

Finally, the Alliance (like individual nation states) has to confront *transnational structures*, particularly of knowledge. To what extent, for example, will the Internet shape NATO's future? Its first use came when the Human Rights Watch criticised NATO's targeting during the Kosovo conflict – and the Serbs used it too, to broadcast their own propaganda (though, it has to be said, with little success).[7] Far more important, though, is likely to be Internet use by NATO's own citizens. Internet users, tracking military forces in a conflict in the future, will be able to switch on not just to a textual account of a campaign or a digital photograph on a screen but to an integrated package offering both. The citizen-sub-scriber will replace the citizen-soldier, and he will be far better informed. He will be able to connect to a computer simulation of a bombing mission and then switch to a live satellite image of a battle zone. Using all the data available, he will be able to email his comments on the operation to the NATO HQ, or the White House and join a chat room of citizens discussing how to prosecute the war. The Internet will do much more than television in involving the citizen as never before in critiquing military operations as they take place.

Taken together, all these factors are indicative of how transnationalism is transforming the strategic context in which decisions are made. They also reveal how military forces are just one element in a patchwork of organisations: relief agencies, civil police, human-rights investigators, and the many interim administrations that now underwrite international security. In this context NATO is an asset-provider, but it is not necessarily the leader. Each of these groups is linked in a synergistic relationship with each other. Security is increasingly shared.

NATO as a Risk Community

Transnationalism is only one feature of NATO's evolution since 1991. Another is the fact that it is in the process of evolving into something generically different from the organisation that we know from the Cold War. It is becoming more responsive not only to transnational factors and concerns but also to the problem of risks.

Benedict Anderson taught us that nations are 'imagined communities'; a nation must first exist in the minds of its citizens before it can hold together on the battlefield or the football terraces. The Cold War saw the emergence of two international communities and the re-imagining of nations that made them up. The most successful act of invention was in Europe, with both Germany and France reinventing themselves as Europeans. 'Anyone who wants to be a German must first become a European', declared Franz Josef Strauss in the 1950s.[8] The new Germany became a civilian power with a strong emphasis on equality and social and civil rights. Even more of a break with the past was its evolution into an anti-Bismarckian state that measured its success in the marketplace, not on the battlefield.

The second Western invention in this period was NATO. This was the first time that it was possible to imagine a Western security community, the arm of Western civilisation. For a time there was even talk of creating an Atlantic Community, with its own executive and legislative institutions.

In our globalised age the idea of 'imagined communities' has been extended globally. It now encompasses what Arjun Appadurai calls other 'imagined worlds' or landscapes. Appadurai talks of a 'historically situated imagination' of the people who inhabit them, and attributes them largely to the force of globalisation. The four kinds of community he identifies are 'ethno-scapes', which refer to the socio-spatial maps of mobile persons (tourists, immigrants, refugees and guest workers) who straddle places and communities; the 'finance-scapes' of global capital and currency markets and the stock exchanges of the world; the 'media-scapes' of electronically produced information and the images of the world disseminated by them; and 'ideo-scapes', the political ideologies of social movements and anti-globalisation protesters.[9] All these imagined spheres are shaping the perceptions of their respective members; they are moulding their view of their globalised world.

Can we add 'securi-scapes' to the list? And, if so, what would they look like? In the 1950s Karl Deutsch described NATO as a 'security community', a community which generated security by integrating its members into a close-knit alliance, a social grouping whose members dealt with each other peacefully. Deutsch applied a typically sociological concept, 'community', to the international arena, arguing, contrary to classical International Relations theory, that a community could exist not only within the boundaries of a state but also across states.[10] Security communities, he argued, share common norms, values and political institutions. Their main function is to keep the peace between its members. And NATO is *still* committed to that mission. After the Kosovo War the NATO Secretary General, Javier Solana, maintained that the operation should be seen as a commitment to 'the further development of peaceful and friendly international relations of the NATO members themselves enshrined in Article 2 of the Washington Treaty'.[11]

Today, however, the condition of peace is largely taken as a given. NATO could be more accurately described as a risk community that secures the interests of its members against the new global insecurity they face. As Beck writes, the world is no longer made up of regional groups but of socio-scapes, or post-national communities that share risks.[12] Although he doesn't use the term 'securi-scape', the term seems a more useful one than Deutsch's concept of a 'security community', for it captures the flavour and immediacy of the risk environment which NATO's Security Concept identified in November 1991 – a 'new security environment' constituted not only by immediate threats (of which there were at the time few) but unnamed 'security challenges and risks'. Eight years later the revised Concept declared that the security of the Alliance was threatened by a wide variety of risks which were often 'multi-directional' and increasingly difficult to predict. They included 'uncertainty and instability in and around the Euro-Atlantic area ... [which] could evolve rapidly'.[13] Clearly, NATO has tried to escape the strictly realist logic of the balance of power, which predicted its disintegration after the Cold War in the absence of any enemy to counterbalance.

Today the perception of risk has replaced the immediate threats of the past. Thus the problem of refugees is becoming vitally important. In August 2001 Britain's Foreign Secretary justified the Kosovo intervention by claiming that half the asylum-seekers in the country that year had arrived as a result of the international community's failure to act decisively in Bosnia in the early 1990s.[14] Other global risks are casting a shadow. In 1996 NATO hosted a major international conference on the safety of blood transfusions in battle zones and the importance of maintaining non-contaminated deep-freeze-stored blood for use by member states in future peacekeeping operations.[15]

Even in the way they conduct war the individual members of the Alliance are distributing risks by contracting out to the private sector. And the same is true of peacekeeping. In Kosovo 16 private companies were involved in clearing the country of mines and unexploded cluster bombs; these ranged from NGOs performing a public service to private companies who were working for profit. Cluster bombs, in fact, are far more deadly than land-mines – when hidden (and in Kosovo 10% failed to go off) they are far harder to detect and dispose of. But even de-mining has its risks. As of 1998, in the American sector of liberated Kuwait 84 contract de-miners had been killed (more than the number of US soldiers killed in combat by enemy fire in the Gulf War).[16]

But there is more to risk than that. Globalisation has ensured that the risks specific to communities are mediated by values. 'Risks cannot be understood,' writes one analyst, 'outside their materialisation in particular mediations, be they scientific, political, economic or popular'.[17] What the West considers a risk will be moulded by its values and norms, by its own way of life – for risks, like anxieties, do not exist independently of our perceptions of them. NATO is not so much a 'securi-scape', then, as it is a risk *community*, because of the values its members have in common.

But it is because risks (though real enough) are also social constructs that they are contested. Whether we think them significant or not, or see them as long-term or short-term, will rest on judgements of their potential. For risks are often 'virtual': they are real in principle, but have yet to materialise in practice. The sociology of risk is the science of potentialities and judgements about probabilities. And this may raise unique problems of its own. Indeed, in protecting a unique way of life the Western community confronts two challenges.

The Precautionary Principle
In 1997 the United States' *National Security Strategy for a New Century* declared one of the principal aims of a security policy should be 'to prevent, disrupt and defeat terrorist operations before they occur'. This principle is embodied in environmental law. A variety of precautionary principles are in use ranging from soft to strong formulations. A relatively soft formulation appears in the 1992 Rio *Declaration on Environment and Development*, which states that:

> *to protect the environment a precautionary approach should be widely applied by states according to their capabilities. Where there are threats of serious or irreversible damage, lack of full scientific certainty shall not be used as a reason for postponing cost-effective measures to prevent environmental degradation.*

In other words, regulators can take cost-effective steps to prevent serious or irreversible harm, even when there is no certainty that such harm will occur.

A stronger formulation is set out in the 2000 Cartagena *Protocol on Bio-safety*, which states that:

> *lack of scientific certainty due to insufficient ... knowledge regarding the extent of the potential adverse effects of living, modified organisms on the conservation and sustainable use*

of biological diversity in the party of import, taking also into account risks to human health, shall not prevent that party from taking a decision as appropriate with regard to the import of the living modified organisms in question ... to avoid or minimise such potential adverse effects.

This formulation drops the requirement for prevention to be cost-effective and shifts the burden of proof for safety onto exporting countries.[18]

When dealing with threats such as terrorism, risk communities too may find the 'precautionary principle' attractive – the consensus that whenever a threat arises it is important that precautions be taken against it. The case made by the United States for attacking the Taliban specifically invoked the concept of 'anticipatory self-defence' (the right to defend itself against anticipated attacks in the future, a new concept that many Americans would like to see enshrined in international law). Thus, the importance attached to positive proof that bin Laden was responsible for the World Trade Center attack, which led the Alliance to invoke Article Five of the Washington Treaty for the first time in its history, may no longer be required in the future.

The problem is compounded by the fact that risk communities are predisposed to engage not in deterrence but in dissuasion. States may be increasingly inclined to threaten others in a different way from the past: not so much 'if you do this, such an action will happen' as 'if you don't do this the consequences could be dire'. Wasn't that exactly the principle of the US action against the Taliban? In a proactive and pre-emptive age the Alliance may no longer react to threats so much as attempt to pre-empt them. Whether the Europeans could be brought round to endorse this – on all or any occasions – is a moot point.

The Risk Trap

Another reason the United States and Europe may find themselves in conflict in future is inherent in the risk society itself. For risk communities have no way of testing the adequacy of the response to a particular problem, such as missile defence and proliferation. Once they know the risk, they have to take a decision: whether to build a defence shield or not – and that is purely a matter of expert opinion, and no two experts can ever agree.

Risks only suggest what should *not* be done rather than what should be done. Doing nothing and demanding too much both transform the world into a series of intractable risks. This is what sociologists call the 'risk trap'.[19] There are no prescriptions for how to act in a risk trap, but there are antithetical cultural reactions. In the case of missile defence the United States has come to the conclusion that it would incur more of a risk if it did not build; Europe (no less threatened) seems to be more impressed by the risks of breaking the conventions against missile defence. And no doubt the Americans are weighing up the risks of finding them-selves in alliance with countries that are likely to respond less positively than they in the face of a missile threat.

It is still possible, of course, that Europe will adopt its own missile defence system sooner rather than later. At a NATO sum-mit in 2001 the Italian Prime Minister told his colleagues that missile defence could possibly be a common project. Spain is installing the *Aegis* weapon system on its F-100 frigates; Italy is co-producing the *Principal* anti-air missile system featuring the *Aster*-A short-range interceptor. These could all provide a point of departure for European collaboration with the United States in constructing a missile defence system of its own.[20] But the National Missile Defense issue also is much more likely to divide than to unite the risk community that NATO is in the process of becoming. The Alliance may only hold together if the United States recognises that the risks are global and cannot be met by a unilateral response. If, on the other hand, it feels that a 'local' response would be preferable, then the risk community faces the threat of breaking up. It is a feature of risk communities that everything is contested – but the more things are contested, the less of a community it will appear to itself, if not the outside world. If Europe and the United States define risks differently, it is difficult to see how a coalition dynamic could survive for long.

NATO, the Doctrine of International Community and the Dialectics of Globalisation

At the Washington Conference in 1949 one of the participants – the

Belgian Prime Minister, Paul Henri Spaak – called it 'an act of faith in the destiny of western civilisation'.[21] And until the very end of the Cold War the Alliance's 'Western' credentials were constantly reaffirmed: in the Atlantic Declaration of 1974, and most recently in the Transatlantic Declaration of 1990. Even following the collapse of communism some commentators expressed the hope that NATO would remain a Western club. Many commentators saw another *existential* threat to Western values in Islamic fundamentalism. In the event, the February 1995 attempt by the then NATO Secretary General, Willie Claes, to redefine its new mission in terms of that threat met with no support from the Council of Ministers.

Indeed, long before the Cold War had run its course Western intellectuals were beginning to define a doctrine of international community. No critic of NATO, Raymond Aron shared none of his own countrymen's fears of American hegemony or their aversion to Anglo-Saxon universalism, but he recognised that if civilisation itself was to be defended in the future against fundamentalist forces that challenged everything that made life 'civil', the West would have to be less exclusive in its definition. 'The present phase of civilisation is coming to an end,' he predicted in the 1960s, 'and for good or ill humanity is embarking on a new phase', that of forging a single world civilisation for the first time, one truly universal in its appeal.[22] What Aron recognized, even at the height of the Cold War, was that, despite the conflict of rival ideologies, global politics would eventually see a return of culture as a determining factor in the formation of political identity, and that a realist paradigm of politics with its narrow focus on endless conflict would be replaced in a global age by 'cooperative security' (a term not then in fashion): a partnership between different societies.

Thirty years later, in a speech in Aachen, Vaclav Havel insisted that the West should retain a normative identity, 'a metaphysically anchored sense of responsibility'. But the metaphysics of the Alliance could no longer be anti-communism but the doctrine of international community. NATO's task should be to rededicate itself to a different project; to admit that there were values which transcended the West, to find what it had in common with other cultures and 'join forces with them in search for a common moral minimum'.[23] Havel has returned to this theme many times since; in a New Year address in 2001 he regretted the fact that globalisation had not been accompanied by a growing sense of global responsibility. And it was that sense of drift that animated Tony Blair's doctrine of international community, as well as, in a somewhat different form, the UN's 'Year of the Dialogue of Civilisations' (2001). And yet it can be argued that NATO has taken responsibility for what happens in the Balkans (the region most immediately within its action radius) since February 1994, when its planes shot down four Serbian aircraft (its first shots ever fired in anger). The Alliance took another step in this direction when it initiated a major bombing campaign against Serb positions around Sarajevo the following September (its first sustained use of force). With the deployment of the Implementation Force (IFOR) for the Dayton Agreement NATO experienced what its then Secretary-General Javier Solana called 'a turning point'.[24] For the first time in its 47 years it deployed ground forces in an 'out-of-area' theatre, forging in the process a close working relationship with the United Nations, the organisation that still expresses the universal ideal. Later, in Kosovo, it went further still by effectively declaring war on Serbia in defence of the 'moral minimum': the fact that ethnic cleansing could no longer be countenanced in the European state system.

Two months into the war in Afghanistan Blair echoed Havel's plea when he talked of a new 'doctrine of international community' based on the need for all the world's civilizations to defend themselves against enemies, internal and external alike. And it was reiterated by Blair's wish to draw Russia into a new security framework with NATO. His hope was that the North Atlantic Council, with Russia, would take part in decision-making in key areas like terrorism and security.[25] In other words, the Alliance already exists not (as in the past) to make the world 'safe for democracy', but, in addressing the problems of failed states and failing societies, *to make globalisation safe for the world*.

Dialectics of Conflict

Ironically, however, three dialectical relationships of globalisation are likely to generate increasing tension between Europe and the United States. And all three should be taken seriously. For, though it is undesirable that the West should act as a monolithic bloc defending its corner against the non-Western world, and though it is indeed desirable that it should work with partners (especially Russia), it would be fatal if the Western community were to find itself at odds.

Dialectic 1: Universal v. Regional

The first dialectic is the clash between the growing uniformity of international culture, as represented in its institutions (democracy) and even behaviour (state attitudes to human rights), and the continued importance of the regional or local. In many cases there is no contradiction between universalism and localism. It is because human rights are discussed in a particular context (such as East Timor, and not merely Kosovo) that they are acknowledged as universal. But, when they are enforced, the human-rights agenda is shaped quite differently. And this may be of increasing importance to the Alliance now that it has gone into the business of enforcing 'universal' norms of behaviour. In the attempt to *instrumentalise* values, conflict may arise over the traditional division between ends and means.

What we find here is a dialectic between 'globalisation' and 'localisation' – one that is identified in the World Bank's Development Report *Entering the Twenty-First Century* (1999/2000). Globalisation reflects the progressive integration of the world's economies; it requires national governments to reach out to international partners as the best way to manage changes affecting trade, financial flows and the global environment. Localisation, by contrast, reflects a growing desire of people for a greater say in government, and manifests itself in the assertion of regional identity.

In the case of global politics, globalisation requires international conventions on human rights and new institutions such as an International Criminal Court. It requires and produces new norms of 'global governance'. But localisation raises the levels of participation in decision-making (through NGOs, protest groups, anti-globalisation movements), which gives people a greater chance to shape the context of their own lives and, in most cases, their regional environment. And in many cases the same is true of governments as well; as the idea of the regional evolves (argues the World Bank), so governments will become more responsive to the desire for regional governance as well. But, as its report also acknowledges, this dialectical relationship is potentially problematic. For localisation can jeopardise macroeconomic stability. It can also make the global observation and understanding of human rights more difficult too, as long as 'global governance' continues to be plural, fluid and potentially *contested*.

Take, for example, the discourse on the Kosovo war. From the beginning, the Americans spoke the language of human rights: the heritage of the United States, a nation founded by immigrants, the great majority of whom until 1945 had been fleeing from political oppression and economic deprivation in Europe. From the beginning the British also spoke the language of globalisation. In his Chicago speech Blair stressed the importance of the growing interdependence of the world, and throughout the eleven-week conflict he continued to stress that the Alliance was acting in 'the interests of wider humanity'.[26]

Britain's European partners, however, chose to interpret the war in more regional and exclusive terms – in terms of localisation rather than globalisation. The French and Germans, in particular, seemed to be intent on creating a European civil space. The language of French intervention might at times differ from that of its closest ally, Germany, but overall the language was surprisingly similar: both were committed to creating a European civil society, 'a community of shared values'.[27] The Germans, if anything, went further by arguing that they were not at war at all, but were pursuing a 'peace policy' (*Friedenspolitik*): a term that has no meaning outside the European context in which it was formulated. Underlying the analysis of the text was the very important phenomenon that the Europeans saw Kosovo as a European war and were not, therefore, much troubled when challenged about why they had intervened in Kosovo but not East Timor. In crafting their support for the war, Europe's leaders went to great lengths to define a special responsibility. And this, in turn, demands a specific

European defence identity. The fact that the Americans largely ran
the war reanimated the debate on a European *security* and defence
identity. In that respect the conflict marked a definitive landmark
in the process of European integration.

Conversely, the events of 11 September suggest that there
may be a long-term reduction of America's security interests on the
fringes of Europe, as America thinks 'global'. And this may mean
that, however unprepared the Europeans may be, they will have to
think of long-term solutions to their own security. Equally important, adds Anatol Lieven, if the Americans do pull back from areas
like the Balkans, the Europeans may have to enter into their own
bilateral institutional relationship with Russia: the country to
which malcontents or nationalists in south-east Europe may turn,
once the United States has vanished from the scene. In the long-
haul battle of 'civilisation' against 'barbarism' the Europeans can
do little militarily to aid the Americans. What they can do best is
defend their own space.[28]

Dialectic 2: Transnational v. National

We will miss the importance of this if we just leave it at that.
Reinhold Niebuhr called the nation 'the most absolute of all human
associations'.[29] That is no longer the case. It is still, to be sure, the
most important of the many frames of reference we now use to
identify ourselves and others. But if the nation is still alive, the
nation state is in decline. Globalisation has reduced the state's
capacity to shape the nation, and it has encouraged the rise of
non-national frameworks of collective identity: a new cosmopoli-
tanism or global consciousness. The nation may still be a citizen's
primary point of reference but the state and the nation are becoming de-linked. Nations are becoming more than, but also less than,
nation states. Even concepts that were once essential to the co-
hesion of the state – such as class, race and religion – are now of
far greater importance to many citizens than their collective national destiny.

We call these separate identities transnational worlds, and
they are another feature of the transformation of the Westphalian
system. These transnational communities appeared abruptly and

most potently in the student activism of the 1960s, which thrived on networks in Berlin, Paris and Chicago. Today, they take their most immediate form in the protest groups against globalisation that have won their battle honours in the streets of Seattle, Gothenburg and Genoa, or in the younger generation of Muslims, who put their faith before their national identity.

And globalisation is not only changing the social configuration of states, it is also changing the configuration of states themselves. It has given rise to a new kind of entity: the transnational state – a hybrid which does not deprive people of a state but gives them instead the means to confront a globalised world by redefining their place in it. The principle of 'inclusive sovereignty' is a paradoxical one, because it enables self-empowerment through the self-denial of certain powers.[30] The nation states of Europe have been forced, nevertheless, to delegate their instruments of power transnationally in order to increase and renew their capacity to influence events in the world at large. Indeed, for twenty years or longer the transnational states of the European Union have grounded their sovereignty on cooperation. This is as true for the Schengen Agreement, with its open frontiers, as it is for the more recent currency union, in which individual currencies have merged into a single one: the euro. The state is still active and alive, and its much-reported 'death' is exaggerated. Instead, globalisation has given it a renewed lease of life, but in a different form.

Thus, even Jacques Delors no longer talks about a federal Europe but a European federation of nation states, and Jacques Chirac (never a federalist, of course) refers not to the United States of Europe but to a United Europe of states. As the 1990s closed, European governments came round to the view that they, not the European Commission, should be the driving force behind European integration. Of the four initiatives currently being undertaken by the EU – the establishment of the Euro, enlargement, the creation of an EU defence force and the review of immigration and asylum procedures – only enlargement provides a serious role for the Commission.

Of these goals, the quest for a European Security and Defence Identity (ESDI) is likely to take transnationalism still further. In the process transnational states may not surrender their legitimate monopoly of force, but they may find themselves surrendering their right of unilateral recourse to war. The point is captured very well by the German Foreign Minister Joschka Fischer, speaking before he joined the government in 1997:

> *during the Mururoa Confrontation in 1995, Chirac had to recognise that European integration has advanced quite a lot since 1965 and the times of de Gaulle. Atomic weapons testing could no longer be taken for granted.*[31]

Fischer was referring to the consumer boycotts against French goods in Germany which, he claimed, had forced France to cancel further atomic tests in the South Pacific. France might still retain an independent nuclear deterrent but it has already lost its capacity to test its weapons independently of (let alone in defiance of) its partners. It is the necessary price the state pays to retain its 'independence'.

The particular example of the Mururoa atoll tests may be debated, but the general principle is clear enough. And this may pose a dilemma for an alliance which includes not only a set of transnational states but also an avowedly national one. For if transnationalism represents one response to globalisation, unilateralism represents another.

Globalisation may affect the interests and intentions of states, but does it necessarily affect the defining properties of statehood? It may have changed the character of international politics by reducing the scope of state activities – or in some cases extending them – but it has not diminished the power of every state to act unilaterally if necessary. In the context of 'global governance' three parallel processes seem to be at work, each working simultaneously. One is multilateralism, increased cooperation between states; another is internationalism, the joint effort by states to make international rules more like domestic ones. The third is unilateralism by states still powerful enough to act independently or even in defiance of international opinion (the United States, China and Iran being three, very different, cases).

What so distresses America's NATO partners about the debate on whether to build an anti-missile shield is their suspicion that the US is calling into question all the doctrines on which its defence and their own rested in the Cold War era: deterrence, non-proliferation and counter-proliferation. They believe that the debate already indicates America's loss of confidence in the approach it has espoused since 1945: collective security through multilateral political commitments and international safeguards. One of Madeleine Albright's favourite catchphrases, after all, was 'multilateral if possible, unilateral if necessary',[32] and many Europeans are worried by what they consider the increasing unilateralism of American foreign policy. Unilateral actions include withholding funds from the United Nations; opposing a UN Rapid Reaction Force as well as an International Criminal Court; applying extraterritorial rules contrary to international law (the Helms-Burton Law); independent or unilateral military action against rogue states (Iraq); failure to sign the Anti-Personnel Landmines Treaty; the decision not to ratify the Kyoto Accord; the 1998 Senate decision to reject the Comprehensive Test Ban Treaty. All these are deemed to raise important questions about America's commitment to multilateralism.

The war in Afghanistan has merely raised further questions about it. American re-engagement with the rest of the world has been on its own terms. There is no sign that the United States has been converted to Blair's doctrine of international community, or that the compromises that have been made (such as the payment of the $800 million the US owed to the UN) are the building blocks of a liberal international order. American policy for years to come may be both interventionist and 'unilateral'. Indeed, the reassertion of American power is clearer today than ever, in part because, for the moment at least, it has humiliated radical Islam in a way that it did not in Lebanon in the 1980s. None of this will be welcome news to a Europe that is itself trying to become more self-assertive, or to a country like Britain that, in its advocacy of the war on terrorism, argued that it could be the launch pad for a new push towards global justice. The United States and Europe could well find themselves on a collision course in future unless they attempt to shape an international system in which American predominance could co-exist with a more principled global order.

Dialectic 3: Americanisation and Anti-Americanism

Even in the United States there are far-right critics of globalisation. The self-styled 'patriots' interpret it as a conspiracy that threatens to subordinate America to the tyranny of 'one-world governance'. It is a conspiracy, they claim, that involves international bankers and the super-rich whose wealth enables them to control governments, manipulate economies and exercise world power.

One of the most important critics, Pat Buchanan, has described globalisation as a plot against national identity. He also accused the Clinton administration of wishing to reduce the United States 'to a subsidiary of the new international economic order'.[33] But even if globalisation has now entered the US political debate, in the shape of Robertson's Christian Coalition and Pat Buchanan's frustrated presidential hopes, the American right-wing critique, with its deliberate appeal to republican tradition, has little if any appeal outside the United States itself – and, it has to be said, little appeal within it. The United States, after all, is the greatest locomotive of globalisation and its greatest beneficiary – or, at least, it is seen as such by the rest of the world – and the 'Americanism' that Buchanan and many of the Republican party who voted for Bush are trying to defend is itself seen to be the threat. The enemies that the far right identifies – US bankers and multinational corporations – are seen by non-American opponents of globalisation to be the problem.

By contrast, anti-American feeling in Europe is potentially far more divisive for the Western Alliance. Globalisation tends to concentrate everything – power, information, capital and especially knowledge – and it is reflected in the growing pull of American culture. But the same dynamic also generates a wish to avoid *cultural marginalisation*. At the popular level this explains why angry mobs attacked the 50 McDonald's restaurants throughout Serbia immediately after the first American cruise missiles struck in the Kosovo War.[34] At a more sophisticated level, even moderate bankers such as Jean-Claude Trichet (the governor of the Banque de France) regularly invoke the now-familiar epithet 'the American hyperpower'.[35]

Anti-Americanism, of course, has been a central theme of European politics since Jean-Jacques Servan-Schreiber in the early

1960s railed against 'le défi Américain', the onslaught of US multinational corporations which, he claimed, were threatening to leave European sovereignty at the mercy of organisations that were both unaccountable and non-transparent. Today the threat is more social than economic, and it appears to be more threatening still for it is threatening to dispossess Europe of its soul.

If many French intellectuals dislike what they call 'the American empire', that is because they see it as a cultural empire above all else. English has become the world's second language; some 350 million people are native speakers, but an additional 1 billion speak enough to strike a bargain or argue the toss about a football game. In 1999 72% of television dramas exported worldwide came from the United States, and immigrants arrive in that country having already lived much of their imaginary lives between New York and Los Angeles. All this leads people to suspect that the American writ runs everywhere – not governing the world but setting the terms on which its governance will take place in the twenty-first century.

And the Europeans have more reason than most to resent this. For what many of them dislike most is the American social model, which differs so markedly from the social democratic model they pioneered in the 1950s, a model which appears to be under threat from globalisation. And what they dislike most about the American model is what they assume it promotes: the intensification of social atomisation, the 'mercantilism' of social relationships, and the tolerance of what are taken to be gross social inequalities, such as the fact that 40% of children in the US now live on the poverty line.[36] This unease may well be manifested in a new critique of NATO, and there are a variety of critics who are already making their views heard. Put another way, the new post-1991 Alliance is summoning up new opposition as the Alliance itself becomes associated with globalisation, Americanisation or an unregulated capitalist market (although there is a tendency for all three to merge into each other in popular discourse).

For globalisation is unsettling, even for those who would not dream of taking to the streets:

> *The threats, real and imagined, to national and local cultures, are widely felt. So too, are the unnerving shifts in the boundaries between governments, business and multi-lateral institutions. As consumers we are stronger, as citizens weaker.*[37]

It is this concern which motivates many of the anti-globalisation protest groups, and which may also alienate many citizens from NATO, now that it is becoming commonplace to identify the Alliance with globalisation (as was the case in many protests against the Afghanistan war).

Let me identify three critiques associated with these movements, which *The Economist* described as 'an ideological rump', 'a coalition of populist conservatives, assorted communitarians and the old Left'.[38] But what may have been a rump is now beginning to coalesce into a movement that we had better take seriously. For the protestors who take to the streets at international meetings are not a mere anomaly; they are the potential harbingers of what Henry Kissinger calls 'a new radicalism' that could threaten the global order.[39]

Conservative Nationalists

Conservative protectionists bewail the declining significance of the national dimension. In part this is because they have had primarily an economic consciousness of themselves. Deutschmark nationalism or 'the export nation' have had an abiding impact on the popular consciousness. Many conservatives now feel threatened by political and cultural devaluation as well.

When it comes to civic consciousness national preferences are still crucial. Opposition to the Kosovo war was mostly a phenomenon of the European Right rather than the Left, although at times both were critical of what they regarded as a feature of America's human-rights agenda. Many conservatives would have been appalled by Vaclav Havel's claim as the war with Serbia went into its third week that the 'transnational moral order' overrode the monopoly of violence by the state, a claim that appeared in an essay entitled provocatively, 'The End of the Nation State'.[40] Conservative opposition to NATO is likely to remain the response of those who remain culturally or ideationally tied to the primacy of the nation state and remain inherently distrustful of any moral interventionism which smacks to them of an American human-rights agenda.

Green Radicals

The critique of the European Left is likely to be found in two other forms of dissent. The first represents a principled and consistent opposition to the use of force in any circumstances. Others in the Green Movement are especially critical of NATO's 'military humanism' as a consensual principle around which the Alliance may reformulate itself in future.[41] Joschka Fischer's principal point of disagreement with his fellow Greens during Kosovo was that for the first time a moral debate had emerged out of a NATO military action. In 1997, with reference to his own party's distrust of the Euro and economic integration, he told them much the same thing: the debate, at least, had begun. 'I share the reservation that Europe is being built around a bank, but, at least its construction will prompt a debate about the definition of a basic European law'.[42]

Fischer himself may also share a reservation against Europe building itself around a defence community, but he probably draws comfort from the fact that the attempt may reopen the debate about a definition of Europe itself. Is it a military power or a 'civilian power' – a term first employed in the early 1970s. A civilian power today may no longer be, as in the past, an anti-military power so much as one that fights only for civility and civilians, or only engages in humanitarian wars. Precisely because of its past, Fischer told the Greens, Germany had only engaged in humanitarian missions from Kosovo to Macedonia (where it became leader of the military force in 2001). Because of its past, Germany is now obliged to join the disinterested coalition wars of the twenty-first century.

Red Dissidents

Then there are the Red dissidents, those who still talk the language of class struggle. They have always seen NATO as the military arm of the rich, but the terms of their critique may change. No longer will they focus on the Cold War divide between the First and

Second Worlds (between West and East) but increasingly on the divide between the First and the Third.

This is of concern even to the most avid globalisers. In the annual contribution to the opinion page of the *International Herald Tribune* highlighting the theme of each year's World Economic Forum at Davos, both its President, Klaus Schwab, and its Managing Director, Claude Smadja, struck a note of urgency:

> *If we do not invent ways to make globalisation more inclusive we have to face the prospect of a resurgence of the acute social confrontations of the past, now magnified at the international level.*[43]

That is why *Le Monde* congratulated the public-sector strikers in 1995 for staging the first 'popular revolt against globalisation'.[44] Even the *New York Times* described the Seattle riots (1999) as the first 'coming out party' for global activism.[45] The fact that many of these movements are often intellectually incoherent should not blind us to their importance. What many (though not all) have in common is a distaste for the polarisation between the globalised rich and a localised poor.

And that is a problem for the Western Alliance. The widening gap between the First and Third Worlds, or between the post-modern and the modern, is likely to grow wider in future. For they are not only two worlds but two existences, as Zygmunt Bauman reminds us. Both revolve around the concept of 'freedom', but not the freedom that the West was in the business of defending during the Cold War. The Western world has freedom: the freedom to move, to trade, to invest capital, to work wherever one pleases. It has the ultimate freedom to act, to make its own future. The non-Western world, represented by Africa and the Middle East, has no future, no sense of agency and no mobility. The First World is mobile; space is traversed in both its real and 'virtual' renditions; the Third World is tied locally, and when it is on the move, movement takes the form of immigration or asylum-seeking.[46] As a State Department official observed, the West urgently needs to put 'a human face on the global economy'[47]– and that may mean being more responsive to the problems of social inequality to be found on NATO's own doorstep: the Mediterranean.

Europe is faced with a demographic crisis, and North Africa with a potential demographic disaster. On current projections North Africa's population will double in the next twenty-five years. Within fifty years Europe will need an additional workforce of 135 million – the figure may be on the high side but the problem is real enough.[48] The Mediterranean is no longer a flank, as it was in the Cold War; it has become an 'interface' between two different cultures or ways of life. It is an interface that has spawned three institutional frameworks for cooperation:

- a Western Mediterranean Forum
- a Mediterranean Council
- the Conference for Security and Cooperation in the Mediterranean, launched by the Italian and Spanish governments in September 1990.

The third framework is the most comprehensive, providing for regional cooperation around three issue areas: security; economics and trade; and cultural and social matters. The question that increasingly has to be asked is whether these initiatives can be synchronised. And they will need to be. If the situation is not handled well, the political leadership of the Alliance might find itself engaged in battles with its critics for the moral high ground that are likely to be just as identity-defining as the great battles against the Peace Movement in the 1950s and 1980s. For, like it or not, the Alliance is in the business of globalisation. That is the ground it has begun to stake out, and the ground on which it will have to fight its battles in the future.

Conclusion

More than a century and a half ago, in his essay, 'Signs of the Time', Thomas Carlyle sought to discern the shape of his own time, the early nineteenth century. He wrote: 'Were we required to characterise this age of ours by any single epithet we should be tempted to call it above all others ... the mechanical age'. Today the spirit of the time (the *Zeitgeist*) is pointing us towards a new goal, for ours is an age of globalisation.

In such an age there is an urgent need to address the security dimension – and, even more urgent, to acknowledge there is one. To do so, in fact, would be one way of reintroducing the political into our thinking and reassuring our citizens that there is still a political realm in which their anxieties can be addressed. In this respect the United States and Europe, as the most globalised societies, need to develop three strategies, one long-term, the others short-term.

Core Strategy[1]

The first and most important is to oppose those who preach the end of politics. They come in many guises. Some focus on ideology, others on economics, others on cultural identity.

For ideological 'endists', the fall of communism has inaugurated a new era in global history marked by the final and irreversible victory of liberalism. There may be some resistance inspired by religious fundamentalism or ethnicity, but these are, by definition, local and without meaning for humanity at large. The melt-down in the Balkans does not challenge the global trends; it throws them into sharp relief. Economic 'endists' reach the same conclusion by a different route. Globalisation has made the state a subsidiary of the marketplace. The only important question for governments is how best to manage those changes – which is a technical question, not a political one. Finally, cultural 'endists' argue that the world is becoming homogenised (or Americanised). In our post-modern, multi-cultural societies, all traditions are crumbling; identities are too fluid to sustain communities of any kind.

All of these should be worrying claims, because they suggest politics is dead: all that is left is economic growth and the pursuit of private interests. These claims also happen to be wrong. As long as ways of life, experiences and values differ, ideological contests are possible. Economically, globalisation is a fact but not a fate. Markets are created through politics, and that is true of global markets too. It is possible that a recession or global meltdown could lead people and governments to react unfavourably, to close off the open-market system as they did in the 1930s.

Indeed, the global economic integration of the late nineteenth and early twentieth centuries ended in the chaos of two world wars and an intervening great depression. But, even before that, the rise of an array of collectivist ideas – nationalism, imperialism, socialism, communism, fascism – did much to undermine belief in a liberal world economy. Similar forces are seen at work today: anti-globalisation protesters provide the anti-liberal fervour, financial markets the economic instability, terrorism the conflict.

The principal lesson of history is that freedom depends on human agency through political institutions. Ironically, the primacy of politics is increasingly acknowledged by many bankers and economists themselves, who since the late 1990s have begun to warn that globalisation is likely to have political consequences that may determine its course in the future. Political protest movements might be strong enough to arrest it, if not put it into reverse, just as economic nationalism and protectionism in the early 1930s changed the global landscape and led to war.

George Soros addresses this question directly in *The Crisis of Global Capitalism*:

> *I can already discern the makings of a final crisis. It will be*
> *political in character. Indigenous political movements are*
> *likely to arise that will seek to expropriate the multinational*
> *corporations and recapture national 'wealth'. Some of them*
> *may succeed in the manner of the Boxer Rebellion or the*
> *Zapatista Revolution. Their success may then shake the*
> *confidence of financial markets engendering a self-reinforc-*
> *ing process.*[2]

For its part, the West, too, needs to see globalisation in political terms and work out political strategies to deal with its challenges and threats.

It does not need to work through NATO, of course. The Western Alliance is greater than any of the institutions that embody it. And there has been a tendency since the war in Afghanistan to dismiss the Alliance as incidental. Defending its 'absence' from the war, George Robertson called it 'relevant', not vital or irreplaceable.[3] And, to be sure, in the 'war against terrorism' the US clearly preferred not only to call the shots but also fire them, free of the messiness of joint command.

It is possible, after NATO's Prague summit in November 2002, that instead of preserving the Alliance's integrated command and control capabilities the United States might be tempted to engage in 'asset stripping' – to use its allies' assets on a selective, bilateral, state-to-state basis. But it would be absurdly premature to write off NATO yet; the Alliance could play a political role in a global age as a rule-altering institution. 'The new strategic environment,' Robertson declared in his Mountbatten Lecture in Edinburgh, 'offers us a unique luxury: the opportunity to set the security agenda ourselves'.[4] It is an opportunity that needs to be seized if NATO is to confront the challenge of the anti-globalisation movement.

Environment Shaping

As George Robertson also remarked in his Mountbatten Lecture, 'security in Europe is a work in progress'.[5] And if that is true of Europe, it is certainly true of the world at large. One of the main objectives for the Western community is to ensure that globalisation continues but that it does so in a way consistent with the interests and values of our own citizens. That means pursuing long-term political strategies to address the sources of conflict and instability in the world.

One example is the proposal of Britain's Chancellor of the Exchequer in November 2001 for a new Marshall Plan to eliminate the most egregious effects of global poverty, especially of education and health, within 20 years. This plan would include the doubling of Western development aid to $100 billion a year. But, critically, it would additionally involve not only a major reform of international institutions but also dramatic changes in the way that developing countries manage their own economic affairs and treat their poorest citizens.[6]

Governments must be held accountable for their actions in every realm if the security environment is to be shaped in a positive fashion. To the discomfort of a number of dictators, the principle of universal jurisdiction over crimes against humanity in national courts is increasingly being recognised. In such ways the institutional outlines of a new international regime can be discerned, though it remains unclear how easily this emerging system can be squared with the realities of international politics, and thus whether it can deliver on its animating promise of ending 'the culture of impunity'.

And, in addressing human security concerns, governments must be more proactive. Security perceptions are now increasingly driven by concerns about personal security – as witness the exponential rise in private security companies whose employees now outnumber the police in most Western societies. The chief targets of global terrorist groups are individuals, not states, or even state interests. Governments must reassure their citizens by following more proactive strategies.

As America's *National Security Strategy for a New Century* declares, the aim should be 'to prevent, disrupt and defeat terrorist operations before they occur'.[7] We should target terrorist funding and networks and be more active in shutting down financial sources, especially the financial links between terrorism and organised crime. Criminal actions could be made more transparent and international cooperation (still lamentably low) could be tightened up.

Hedging Strategy

By defining the post-Cold War security environment in terms of 'security challenges and risks', NATO has redefined a rule-directing Western security policy in terms of the management of risks. Should that management fail, of course, the West needs to hedge against disasters, given their global nature. It needs in place forces that could act in a more concerted way than NATO did after the events of 11 September. It needs a more broad-based strategy with regard to Madeleine Albright's 'force multiplier', the partnership between the public, private and voluntary sectors in dealing with humanitarian crises that are likely to further destabilise the world and promote insecurity in Western Europe.

It also needs to investigate more thoroughly how NATO's contributions for combat, peacekeeping and humanitarian operations might be utilised more effectively. By exploring a NATO–Russia contingency command HQ concept in several locations, including Russia, and inclusive of NATO, EU and non-NATO Partnership for Peace (PFP) and Mediterranean Dialogue countries, the Alliance could in the future confront global threats more functionally.[8]

In the end, of course, these are all daunting challenges. And we should not underestimate the difficulty of sustaining international coalitions among states that are still culturally different from each other. It usually goes unremarked that how globalised we are depends on our response to globalisation. Globalisation changes not only material structures like states and security communities, but also the structure of time and space, and thus the way we conceive of both and our place in them. But it is precisely because the West is the most globalised community that it has no option but to take the lead.

Notes

Introduction

[1] Globalisation appeared first in 1961: see *Webster's Third New International Dictionary of the English Language* (Springfield, MA: Merriam, 1961). Academically, the term first entered the social sciences in the 1980s, pioneered by Roland Robertson and Anthony Giddens. Malcolm Waters calls both the fathers of globalisation; see Malcolm Waters, *Globalisation* (London: Routledge, 1995).

Chapter 1

[1] Mark Rupert, *Ideologies of Globalisation: Contending Visions of a New World Order* (London: Routledge, 2000), p. 46.

[2] World Bank, *World Economic Report 1999/2000* (Washington DC: 2000).

[3] Pierre Hassner 'Beyond War and Totalitarianism: The New Dynamics of Violence', in Gwyn Prins and Hylke Tromp (eds), *The Future of War* (The Hague: Kluwer Law, 2000), pp. 197–213; Samuel Huntingdon, *Clash of Civilisations* (New York: Simon & Schuster,

1996), p. 68; Mary Kaldor, *New and Old Wars: Organised Violence in the Global Era* (Cambridge: Polity Press, 1999).

[4] Cited in Manfred Kossok, 'From Universal History to Global History', in Bruce Mazlish and Ralph Bultjens (eds), *Conceptualising Global History* (Boulder, CO: Westview Press, 1993), p. 96.

[5] Brian C. Schmidt, *The Political Discourse of Anarchy: A Disciplinary History of International Relations* (Albany, NY: State University of New York Press, 1998), p. 70.

[6] Andrew Linklater, 'The Problem of Harm in World Politics', Martin Wight Lecture, 20 November 2001, p. 14 (unpublished paper).

[7] Zygmunt Bauman, *Life in Fragments* (Oxford: Blackwell, 1995), p. 24.

[8] Katerina Dalacoura, 'Islamicist Movements as Non-state Actors and Their Relevance to International Relations', in Daphne Josselin and William Wallace (eds), *Non-state Actors in World Politics* (London: Palgrave, 2001), p. 247.

[9] Ali Mazrui, *Cultural Forces in World Politics* (London: James Currey, 1990), pp. 224–5.

[10] Michael Ignatieff, *The Need of Strangers*, cited in Joseph Amato, *Victims and Values* (Boulder, CO: Praeger, 1990), p. 199.

[11] Ian Clark, *Globalisation and International Relations Theory* (Oxford: Oxford University Press, 1999), p. 1. For commodity and financial markets, see also Michael D. Bordo and Douglas A. Irwin, 'Is Globalisation Today Really Different from Globalisation a Hundred Years Ago?', *Brookings Trade Forum 1999* (Washington DC: Brookings Institution, 1999), pp. 1–50.

[12] Roland Robertson, *Globalisation: Social Theory and Global Culture* (London: Sage, 1992).

[13] Martin Albrow, *The Global Age: State and Society Beyond Modernity* (Cambridge: Polity Press, 1996), p. 119.

[14] World Trade Organisation (WTO) 'Ruggiero calls for the trading system to be kept in line with globalisation process', WTO Press Release, 22 February 1996.

[15] Robert Kaplan, *Warrior Politics* (New York: Random House, 2002), p. 5.

Chapter 2

[1] Max Singer and Aaron Wildawsky, *The Real World Order: Zones of Peace, Zones of Turmoil* (Chatham, NJ: Chatham Publishers, 1991), p. 3.

[2] Joseph Nye, 'Military De-globalisation?', *Foreign Policy*, January/February 2001, pp. 82–3.

[3] Jan Aart Scholte, *Globalisation: A Critical Introduction* (London: Palgrave, 2000), p. 33.

[4] See Tanja Ellingsen, 'Colourful Community or Ethnic Witches' Brew?', *Journal of Conflict Resolution*, vol. 44, no. 2 (April, 2000), p. 243. Paul Collier, 'Doing Well Out Of War: An Economic Perspective', in Mats Berdal and David Malone (eds), *Greed and Grievance: Economic Agendas in Civil Wars* (Boulder, CO: Lynne Rienner, 2000), p. 97.

[5] Mary Kaldor, *New and Old Wars: Organised Violence in the Global Era* (Cambridge: Polity Press, 1999), p. 70.

[6] I.W. Zartman, ' Introduction: Posing the Problem of State Collapse', in I.W. Zartman (ed.), *Collapsed States: The Disintegration and Restoration of Legitimate Authority* (Boulder, CO: Lynne Rienner, 1995), p. 2.

[7] Martin Shaw, *Post-military Society: Militarism, Demilitarisation and War at the End of the Twentieth Century* (Cambridge, Polity Press, 1991), p. 38.

[8] Cited in Hassner, *op. cit.*, p. 204.

[9] Cited in *Ibid.*

[10] Cited in *Ibid.*

[11] Yahya Sadowski, *The Myth of Global Chaos* (Washington DC: Brookings Institution, 1998), p. 38.

[12] John Keegan, *The Spectator*, 16 April 1998.

[13] Charles King, 'Trouble in the Balkans', *Times Literary Supplement*, 20 July 2001, p. 3. For a convincing critique of the 'new war' school, see Mats Berdal, 'How "New" Are '"New" Wars? Reflections on Global Economic Change and War in the Early Twenty-first Century', unpublished paper prepared for the 43rd annual IISS Conference (2001).

[14] Howard Temperley, *British Antislavery, 1833–1870* (London: Longman, 1972). The *Economist* article appeared on 26 February 1848. I am grateful to Paul Kliestra for this reference.

[15] John Keane, 'Who's In Charge Here?', *Times Literary Supplement*, 28 May 2001, p. 14.

[16] *Ibid.*, p. 15.

17 'There's nothing just or unjust which does not change with the climate' (Pascal, *Pensées*), cited in Villiers de l'Isle-Adam, *Cruel Tales* (Oxford: Oxford University Press, 1985), p. 258.

18 Manuel Castells, *The Internet Galaxy* (Oxford: Oxford University Press, 2001), p. 139.

19 Kenneth Anderson, 'Language, Law and Terror', *Times Literary Supplement*, 21 September 2001, p. 15. See also Howard Cargill, 'Perpetual Peace? Kosovo and the Elision of Police and Military Violence', *European Journal of Social Theory*, vol. 4, no. 1, February 2001, pp. 74–6.

Chapter 3

1 Cited Carl E. Schorske, *Thinking with History: Explorations in the Passage of Modernism* (Princeton, NJ: Princeton University Press, 1998), p. 191.

2 Secretary of State Colin Powell, 'Remarks to United Nations General Assembly', address at Special Session on HIV/AIDS, New York, 25 June 2001.

3 BBC News, '"War Footing" Urged To Fight AIDS', 12 July 2000, http://news.bbc.co.uk/hi/english/world/newsid_830000/830144.stm.

4 William Fox, 'Phantom Warriors: Disease as a Threat to US National Security', *Parameters*, Winter 1997–8.

5 See NATO/CCMS website: http://www.nato.int/pilot.htm.

6 http://www.denix.osd.mil/denix/Public/news/osd/estic/estic.html.

7 http://www.asq.osd.mil/bmds/bmdolink/hml/supple.html.

8 *International Herald Tribune*, 10 October 1995.

9 'The Alliance as Strategic Concept', NATO Press Release, NAC-S99 (95), 24 April 1999.

10 'Excerpts: Clinton on US National Security Strategy for the Twenty-first Century', *The US Mission to NATO* (Washington DC: State Department, 11 January 2000).

11 Cited in Martin Albrow, *op. cit.*, p. 75.

12 Jim Walsh, 'History Says Hold Fire on Missile Defence', *The Times*, 7 August 2001, p. 12.

13 Kenneth F. McKenzie, 'The Revenge of the Melians: Asymmetric Threats and the Next Quadrennial Defence Review', *McNair Paper* 62 (Washington DC: National Defense University, 2000), p. 20.

14 Daniel Bell, *Sociological Journeys: Essays* (London: Heinemann, 1980).

15 Anthony Brown, 'UN's Smallpox Terror Alert', *The Observer*, 21 October 2001.

16 David Martin Jones and M.L.R. Smith, 'Franchising Terror', *The World Today*, October 2001, p. 11.

17 *Ibid.*

18 Anatol Lieven, 'Strategy for Terror', *Prospect*, October 2001, p. 19.

19 For a discussion of expressive violence, see Anton Blok, 'The Meaning of "Senseless" Violence', in Anton Blok, *Honour and Violence* (Cambridge, Polity Press, 2001), pp. 102–15.

20 Cited in J. Bordo, 'Ecological Peril, Modern Technology in the Post-modern Sublime', in P. Berry and A. Wernick, *Shadow of Spirit: Post-modernism and Religion* (London: Routledge, 1992), p. 168.

21 Jean Chesneaux, *Brave New Modern World: The Prospects for Survival* (London: Thames and Hudson, 1992), p. 56.

22 Brian Fagin, *Floods, Famine and Emperors: El Niño and the Fate of Civilisation* (London: Pimlico, 2000), p. 257.

23 Hugh Dyer, 'Environmental Security in International Relations: The Case for Enclosure', *Review of*

International Studies, vol. 27 (2001), p. 446.

24 Pearson Commission (Commission on International Development), *Partners in Development* (New York: Praeger, 1969).

25 United Nations Development Programme, *UN Human Development Report 1999* (Washington DC: 1999).

26 United Nations Development Programme, *UN Human Development Report 1994* (Washington DC: 1994).

27 Robert Wright, 'Will Globalisation Make You Happy?', *Foreign Policy*, Sept/Oct 2000, pp. 57–8.

28 Contact crimes include assaults and threats, sexual violence and sexual harassment and robbery.

29 United Nations Secretary General Millennium Report, *We The Peoples: The Role of the United Nations in the Twenty-first Century* (New York: March 2000).

30 See Valpy FitzGerald, 'The International Political Economy of Conflict in Poor Countries', in Frances Stewart and Valpy FitzGerald (eds), *War and Underdevelopment*, vol. 1, *The Economic and Social Consequences of Conflict* (Oxford: Oxford University Press, 2001).

31 See Caroline Moorehead 'Fugitive Resentment', *Times Literary Supplement*, 16 November 2001.

32 *Ibid.*

33 *Ibid.*

34 Cited in Phil Marfleet, 'Migration and The Refugee Experience' in Phil Marfleet (ed.), *Globalisation and the Third World* (London: Routledge, 1998), p. 71.

35 Ulrich Beck, *What is Globalisation?* (Cambridge: Polity Press, 2000).

36 Michael Gove, 'Breed or Die Out', *The Times* 15 November 2001, p. 12.

37 Cited in Louise Shelley, 'Transnational Organised Crime: An Imminent Threat to the Nation State', *Journal of International Affairs*, vol. 48, no. 2 (Winter 1995), p. 463. For a further discussion of the crisis in North Africa see Peter Andreas ' Transnational Crime And Economic Globalisation', in Mats Berdal and Monica Serrano (eds), *Business as Usual? Transnational Organised Crime and International Security* (Boulder, CO: Lynne Rienner, 2002).

38 For crime as a national security threat, see R. T. Naylor, 'From Cold War to Crime War: The Search for a New National Security Threat', *Transnational Organised Crime*, vol. 1, no. 4 (Winter 1995), p. 37.

39 Mark Galleoti, 'Underworld and Upperworld: Transnational Organised Crime and Global Society' in Josselin and Wallace, *op. cit.*, p. 203.

40 H. Richard Friman and Peter Andreas (eds) *Illicit Global Economy and State Power* (New York: Rowman & Littlefield, 1999).

41 Galleoti, *op. cit.*, p. 212.

42 *Ibid.*, p. 215.

43 *The Global Infectious Disease Threat and its Implications for the United States*, Report of the US National Intelligence Council, NIC 99–17D, January 2000.

44 Richard Holbrook, 'Ambassador Holbrook testifies to Congress on HIV/AIDS, 8 March 2000' (USIS, Washington File, available at www.regis.com).

45 *The National Security Strategy for a Global Age* (Washington DC: The White House, December 2000), p. 19.

46 *Global Trends 2015: A dialogue About the Future with Non government Experts*, National Intelligence Council, NIC 2000–2002, January 2000.

47 Roxanne Bazergan, 'Testing Times', *The World Today*, May 2001, p. 7.

48 *Global Infectious Disease Threat, op. cit.* For a comprehensive discussion of AIDS, see Stefan Elbe, *The Strategic Dimension of HIV/AIDS*, Adelphi Paper (Oxford: Oxford University Press for the IISS, forthcoming).

49 'Contagion and Conflict: Health as a Global Security Challenge', *Report of the Chemical and Biological Arms Control Institute and CSIS International Security Programme*, January 2000, p. vii.

50 Speech by Tony Blair, Economic Club of Chicago, 'The doctrine of the international community', 22 April 1999, http://www.usis.it/wireless/wf990423/99042319.html.

51 John Keane, *Reflections of Violence* (London: Verso, 1996), p. 120.

52 See www.un.org/moreinfo/ngolink/dsg.38.htm.

53 Ashton Carter and William Perry, *Preventative Defense: A New Security Strategy for America* (Washington DC: Brookings Institution, 1999), p. 18.

54 J. D. Steinbrunner, *Principles of Global Security* (Washington DC: Brookings Institution, 2000), p. 146.

55 Afaf Mahfouz, 'Opening remarks', Conference of NGOs in consultative partnership with the United Nations, 53rd annual DP-NGO Conference, New York, 28 August 2000 (www.conferenceofngos.org/ngomeet/dpingo.htm).

56 *Ibid.*

57 Chad Carpenter, 'Business, Green Groups and the Media: The Role of NGOs in the Climate Change Debate', *International Affairs*, vol. 77, no. 2 (2001), p. 319.

58 See Daniel Byman, 'Uncertain Partners: NGOs and the Military', *Survival*, vol. 43, no. 2 (Summer 2000), pp. 97–114.

59 Cited in T. Gibbings and D. Hurley 'Interagency Operations

Centers: An Opportunity We Cannot Ignore' *Parameters*, Winter 1998, p. 86.

Chapter 4

1 Vaclav Havel, 'The End of the Modern Era', *New York Times*, 1 March 1992 (cited in Mazlish and Bultjens, *op. cit.*, p. 124). 'The era of belief in automatic progress brokered by the scientific method is over'.

2 Cited in Matei Calinescu, *Five Faces of Modernity* (Durham, NC: Duke University Press, 1987), p. 56.

3 Deborah Lipton, *Risk* (London: Routledge, 1999), p. 11.

4 Mary Douglas, *Risk and Blame: Essays in Cultural Theory* (London: Routledge, 1992), p. 15.

5 Ulrich Beck, *World Risk Society* (Cambridge: Polity Press, 1999).

6 *New York Times*, 17 December 1998.

7 Douglas, *op. cit.*, p. 13.

8 *Time*, 28 April 1994.

9 Beck, *World Risk Society, op. cit.*, p. 51.

10 'US tries to get next term target', *Guardian Unlimited*, 3 November 2001 (html:www.theguardian.co.uk/uslatest.story).

11 Cited Kenneth Waltz, 'Globalisation and American Power', *The National Interest*, Spring 2000, p. 56.

12 http://www.dailynews.yahoo.com/h/nm/20010822/ts/balkans-macedonia.dc.37.html.

13 Tony Blair 'Prime Minister's statement on military action in Afghanistan', 7 October 2001 (http://www.numberten.gov.uk/news/asp).

14 Richard Ericson and Kevin Haggerty, *Policing the Risk Society* (Toronto: University of Toronto Press, 1997), p. 41.

15 Wyn Bowen, 'Rogues No More', *The World Today*, August/ September 2000, p. 14.

16 *Washington Post*, 27 February 2001.

17 United Nations, *Report of second panel established pursuant to the note of the President of the Security Council of 30 January 1999 (S/1999/100) concerning the current humanitarian situation in Iraq* (New York: UN, 30 March 1999), http://www.un.org/Depts/oippan el.rep/html.

Chapter 5

1 World Trade Organisation (WTO), *World Trade Statistics 1999–2000* (Geneva: WTO, 2000).

2 Linda Weiss, *The Myth of the Powerless State: Governing the Economy in a Global Era* (Cambridge, Polity Press, 1998), p. 186.

3 http://dictionary.oed.com/cgi/entr y/00256430, transnation.a.(n).

4 James N. Rosenau, *Turbulence in World Politics: A Theory of Change in Continuity* (Princeton, NJ: Princeton University Press, 1990), p. 6.

5 Charles Guthrie, 'Why NATO Cannot Simply March in and Crush Milosevic', *Evening Standard*, 1 April 1999.

6 Cited in Gibbings and Hurley, *op. cit.*, p. 86.

7 James Dunnigan, *Digital Soldiers* (New York: St Martin's Press, 1996), p. 285.

8 Cited in Christopher Coker, *Twilight of the West* (Boulder, CO: Westview, 1998), p. 109.

9 Barry Smart, *Post-Modernity* (London: Routledge, 1993), p. 147.

10 Karl Deutsch, *Political Community in the North Atlantic Area* (Boston: Houghton Mifflin, 1957), p. 5

11 Speech by Dr Javier Solana, NATO Secretary General, International NATO Workshop, Budapest, Hungary, 21 June 1999.

12 Beck, *World Risk Society, op. cit.*, p. 16.

13 NATO Press Release, NAC-S99 (95) 24 April 1999.

14 *The Times*, 29 August 2001.

15 *The Times*, 26 August 1996.

16 See Maxwell Cameron, Robert Lawson and Brian Tomlin (eds) *To Walk Without Fear: The Global Movements to Ban Landmines* (Toronto: Oxford University Press, 1998), p. 321.

17 Beck, *World Risk Society, op. cit.*, p. 136.

18 UNDP, *Human Development Report 2001: Making New Technologies Work for Human Development* (New York: Oxford University Press, 2001), p. 70.

19 Beck, *World Risk Society, op. cit.*, pp. 141–2.

20 David J. Smith, 'Bush European Success Calls for NATO Missile Defence Plan', *Inside Missile Defense*, vol. 7, no. 4 (11 July 2001), p. 3.

21 Cited in Hans Kohn, *Twentieth Century: A Midway Account of the Western World* (London: Gollancz, 1950), pp. 233–4.

22 Cited in Fernand Braudel, *A History of Civilisation* (London: Allen Lane, 1994), p. 8.

23 Vaclav Havel, 'The Hope for Europe', address in Aachen, 15 May 1996, reprinted in *New York Review of Books*, 20 June 1996, p. 38.

24 Douglas Stuart, 'The United States and NATO Out Of Area Disputes', in Gustav Schmidt (ed.), *A History of NATO: The First 50 Years* (London: Palgrave, 2001), p. 137.

25 *The Times* 17 November 2001.

26 Tony Blair, Speech to the Economic Club of Chicago, 'The Doctrine of the International Community', 22 April 1999 (www.usis.it/wireless/wf990423/9 9042319.htm).

27 Government policy statement by Chancellor Gerhard Schroeder, Bonn, 26 March 1999, http://www.bundeskanzler.de/kan zerenglkish/o1,0101/index.html.

28 Anatol Lieven 'The End of NATO,' *Prospect*, December 2001, pp. 14–15.

29 Reinhold Niebuhr, *Moral Man and Immoral Society: A Study in Ethics and Politics* (New York: Scribner, 1932), p. 83.

30 Ulrich Beck, *What is Globalisation?*, *op. cit.*, p. 29.

31 *Ibid.*, p. 158.

32 *The Times*, 22 November 1999.

33 Rupert, *op. cit.*, p. 112.

34 www.salon.com/news/feature/199 9/04/26/belgrade/index1.html.

35 Cited in Beck, *What is Globalisation?*, *op. cit.*, p. 18

36 Zaki Laidi, *A World Without Meaning: Crisis of Meaning in International Politics* (London: Routledge, 1998), pp. 165–6.

37 Philip Stephens, *Financial Times*, 17 August 2001.

38 *The Economist*, 22 June 1998. For the breakdown of Conservatives, Greens, and Reds, see Beck, *What is Globalisation?*, p. 10.

39 Henry Kissinger, *Does America Need a Foreign Policy: Towards a Diplomacy for the Twenty-first Century* (New York: Simon & Schuster, 2001), p. 218.

40 Cited in Oscar Lafontaine, *Das Herz Schlägt Links* (Munich: Econ Verlag, 1999), p. 252.

41 Cited in Noam Chomsky, *The New Military Humanism: Lessons from Kosovo* (London: Pluto Press, 1999).

42 Cited in Beck, *What is Globalisation?*, *op. cit.*, p. 158.

43 Rupert, *op. cit.*, pp. 145–6.

44 *The Times*, 29 September 1995.

45 *New York Times*, 2 December 1999.

46 Zygmunt Baumann, *Globalisation: The Human Consequences* (Cambridge: Polity Press, 1998), p. 28.

47 Halina Ward, 'Corporate Citizenship: an international perspective on the emerging agenda', *Conference Report, June 2000* (London: Royal Institute of International Affairs, 2000), p. 2.

48 George Joffe, 'Europe and the Mediterranean: The Barcelona Process 5 Years On', *Briefing Paper 16* (London: Royal Institute of International Relations, August 2000).

Conclusion

1 This schema is derived from the RAND framework for conceptualising national counter-terrorist strategies. See Ian Lesser, Bruce Hoffman *et al.* (eds) *Countering the New Terrorism* (San Francisco, CA: RAND, 1998).

2 George Soros, *The Crisis of Global Capitalism* (New York: Public Affairs Publishing, 1998), p. 134.

3 *The Times*, 7 December 2001.

4 George Robertson, 'NATO in the New Millennium', Mountbatten Lecture at the University of Edinburgh (Brussels: NATO Office of Information and Press, 2001), p. 1.

5 *Ibid.*, p. 3.

6 Anatol Kaletsky, 'Blair's Optimistic Zeal Was Not Misguided', *The Times*, 22 November 2001, p. 20.

7 Cited in Christopher Harman, *Terrorism Today* (London: Frank Cass, 2000), p. 257.

8 Sean Kay and Josh Spero 'Keep NATO Relevant for the Twenty First Century,' *Defence News*, 17 December 2001.